Family Court Is a F*ck'n Joke

Exposing the Corrupt Family Court System & Navigating Parental Alienation

KENYADA JONES

Published by University of Moguls Publishing

Cover design by University of Moguls Publishing
www.universityofmoguls.com

ISBN-13: 978-1-956134-18-6

For speaking engagements and bulk book orders:
Kenyada Jones
kenyada@mylensmyway.com
866.985.2478

Website:
www.familycourtisajoke.com
Instagram:
@therealkenyadajones
Facebook:
Kenyada Jones

Dedication

This book is dedicated to every alienated parent, grandparent, sibling, family member, and friend.

Acknowledgment

I would like to thank my son, Jahad Jones, for being a shoulder to cry on throughout my entire parental alienation journey. There were times when I took out my frustrations on him when I had no other outlet to vent. He watched and witnessed every step of the roller-coaster ride. He's an alienated brother. He is affected by parental alienation as his relationship with his sister is not the same.

I would like to thank my family and friends who continued to pray and try to provide emotional support as best as they could.

I also would like to thank Sheneice for keeping me inspired to write this book and for all the pointers and tips you shared.

Lastly, I would like to thank my daughter for being the best daughter ever. We will never be able to get back all the time we lost, however, I'm looking forward to creating many new memories. I love you, girl!

Table of Contents

Introduction

According to the National Center for State Courts, "Parental Alienation is a strategy whereby one parent intentionally displays to the child unjustified negativity aimed at the other parent. The purpose of this strategy is to damage the child's relationship with the other parent and to turn the child's emotions against that other parent."

My child was taken from me by family court, attorneys, and a bitter ex. I went from being a proud, loving, active father to a so-called monster of a father that never existed. My book is based on my personal experience with parental alienation. Family court does not acknowledge this as a real thing. "The researchers estimate that twenty-two million American adults, and close to four million children, have been victimized by parental alienating behaviors. They also found that forty-seven percent of moderately to severely alienated parents had contemplated suicide within the past year." (Colorado State University, 2019). "Whether direct or indirect, parental alienation harms families." (Science Daily, 2019). After reading my story, you will become educated about parental alienation, and hopefully you can join me in spreading awareness.

Book Mission:

To raise awareness about parental alienation.

Parental alienation is child abuse. It's the ultimate hate crime targeted against a loving parent. There will come a day when the child realizes that everything one parent said about the other was a lie. According to the *Divorce Corp* documentary, "Family court is a $50-billion-dollar-a-year industry. Corrupt judges have unchecked power over your personal finances and your children's lives." My objective is to make sure that every living person has an understanding of what parental alienation is and the emotional trauma it brings.

To my daughter:

I hope all is well with you. It's been about four years since I've seen you, hugged you, spoke to you, laughed with you, and seen your smile. Your absence from my life is by far my most painful experience ever. I think about you every day, and every day I hope to get a response. I know the day will eventually come. I know you don't fully understand what happened between us, but soon you will start to figure it out and see the truth for yourself. I wrote this book to give you the opportunity to hear my side of the story. I know I scared you that night and said some really mean shit. If you knew what I know, then I'm sure you would understand where all that aggression stemmed from. Hopefully, you'll find clarification in this book.

I'm sure you're still the same silly, quiet, observant, caring, and smart girl I've known since you were born. I miss you like crazy. I just wanted to spend as much time with you as possible, love on you, and watch you grow. I never imagined I'd be punished for it. I cherish all the memories we created and will never forget them. I also look forward to creating new memories as I patiently wait. One day, you will tell your side of the story and how you overcame what you went through, and it will become part of someone else's survival guide.

I love you 4L,
Your Real Dad

Why do alienated parents let go?

"Because they realize what it costs to remain in the nightmare exceeds their emotional, mental and physical resources. And they know their lives are bigger, and they are more deserving than the parental alienation destruction."

– Dr. Jeanne King, PhD

CHAPTER 1

Silent Father Influences

Growing up without a father who was actively present in my life was always difficult for me to understand. New Orleans is a very small city, and just from your last name alone, a random person you meet can know your entire family. If you know, you know. Growing up, I realized most of my friends didn't have their father in their lives either so it became normal to me, to the point where, if a friend did have a father present, it would look and feel strange to be around them. Fortunately, my grandpa, Alfred Parker (resting in peace), and my uncles, Kerry and Marlon, were active in my life. For a few years I was able to witness them raise my younger cousins. Unbeknownst, the seed was planted early through them. Thank you, Unc. I appreciate ya'll.

I was born in the lower 9th Ward (The Desire Housing Projects), where I lived until I was ten years old. When I was twelve, my mom decided to move to Inglewood, California. I can remember being sad because now I'll be without my family and friends. Somewhere during middle school was when I started to realize that something was missing from my life. I believe it started after a friend's mom took me and my friends to see *Boyz n the Hood*. It was definitely the blueprint to the LA lifestyle. The gang culture was definitely new to me, but I was never really afraid because I had already come from a similar culture. The scenes that stood out most were those about Furious and Tre's relationship. This is something I'd never seen before, and it immediately had my attention. I remember saying to myself, *Damn, this nigga mean. LOL.* Now I can LOL for feeling that way, but in the end, Furious had won me over and I could feel what was missing from my life at that point.

I was only twelve and was already feeling like, *This is the kind of father I'mma be when I get older.* I was fortunate enough to have real-life father figures in my early teens. Mr. Felder, the father of my childhood and still bestfriend, Eddie Felder, was one of them. Mr. Felder was the coolest cat ever to me. He dressed sharp as a tac, had a cool li'l bop in his walk, and was always happy. At first, I thought Mr. Felder was weird because when I would go to Eddie's house to play Nintendo he'd be in the kitchen, cookin' up some dinner for him and Eddie. He even made sure I ate when I was there. To me, this was very strange because I had never experienced a single-father scenario. Mr. Felder would take us to school every morning, take us swimming in the summer, and take us to all the school dances—Magic Mountain, parties—you name it, he did it! I mean Mr. Felder was a real Mr. Mom. Furious' style was a little more aggressive than Mr. Felder's, however, I saw the beauty in both. RIP, "good buddy." I appreciate you.

Mr. Crowder, the father of my other childhood and still bestfriend, Jermaine, was my first experience with seeing how a married family functioned. Mr. Crowder was the ol' school, hard-hat-wearing father. He worked for the Los Angeles County Sanitation Department. He worked from 5 a.m. to 2 p.m. every single day for twenty-five-plus years. Jermaine lived in Inglewood also in a nice-sized house, and Mr. Crowder even built a basketball court in the backyard for all of us to hoop and hang out at. I remember saying to myself, *Damn, Jermaine is rich.* Mr. Crowder is a man's man, meaning he don't take no shit! He provided for and protected his family at all costs. He kept a 9mm in his door panel, so don't you dare try to disrespect. He will shoot first and ask questions last. *LOL.* He's also a handyman who specialized in auto mechanics, hunting, and flipping birds. I had never experienced this type of man in my life other than my grandfather, but I was too young to reap the full benefits from him. Mr. Crowder passed on all his characteristics to Jermaine, and we would always tease and call Jermaine "old man" because there we were, thirteen, fourteen years old, and Jermaine would always be the mature, responsible one out of the crew. It wasn't until I was in my early twenties that I realized how much I valued Mr. Crowder. I appreciate you, Mr. Crowder.

Mr. Orange, the father of another childhood and still best friend, Kevin, was also a single father. He was a single father in a live-in relationship with his girlfriend, Evelyn. Evelyn was much younger than Mr. Orange and she was hella fine too. *LOL*. Kevin would always get pissed when we would make sexual comments about her. To us, Evelyn was like Mrs. Parker from *Friday*. Mr. Orange was also a man's man and was one of the most down-to-earth fathers ever. Kevin lived in Hawthorne so on the weekends, we would always catch the 40 bus from Market Street to go hang out at Kevin's crib. Kevin lived across the street from the Hawthorne Mall, so we would always go there to meet girls and take them back to his house. Mr. Orange always knew we were up to something but he never gave us a hard time. He was always a happy-go-lucky man, and he definitely passed that trait down to Kevin. RIP, Mr. Orange. I appreciate you.

Mr. Womack, whom I called Charlie Wo, the father of another best friend of mine, Lamar, was also a single father. He was a single father to three other boys/men in the house. Mr. Womack was aggressive and never held his tongue. Also dressed sharp as tac, he was an old school playa who would always rock a Dobbs hat with the feather on the side. Mr. Womack provided shelter for all of his sons, and I mean these are some big ass boys. The Womack house was very aggressive but it never was a question who the big dog was, and the respect in his home was mandatory. I didn't spend much time with Mr. Womack, but when I did, he always made his presence felt. RIP, Charlie Wo. I appreciate you.

These men helped me to create an image in my mind of what kind of father I wanted to be. I saw the beauty in all of their personalities and eventually applied some of it once I became a father. At that point, I began to develop strong feelings of hate and resentment towards my own father. At first, I believed it was normal for kids not to have their fathers because that's mostly what I experienced growing up, but I started to see things differently. I thought to myself, *How can a man father a child and not be present in his life?* I remember my first time hearing "Be a Father to Your Child" by Ed O.G. and Da Bulldogs and wondered if my father ever heard it and how he'd react to it if he did. My father would call me from time to time, and even though I had no respect for him, from the inside I was kinda happy to hear his voice. I see a lot of his characteristics in me, and I just couldn't understand why he was not there.

Neither my mother or my grandmother would ever say anything bad about him to me. They would never speak bad on him and would always ask me if I had heard from him. Of course, there were occasions when I'd get in an argument with my mom and say something like, "I wanna go live with my dad," and she would say something slick like, "Well, go call him and tell him to come get you!" I'm sure she already knew that wasn't happening. There was never a time when I felt like my mom was trying to turn me against him. I always realized it was all on him. Him not being there made me feel empty inside, and I hated him for that.

As I was getting older, I'd ask my mom questions about his background, and that was when I found out that he was a marine veteran. She'd tell me how cool of a guy he was in high school. He was a high school basketball star with a bright future, but that all ended with some kind of leg or ankle injury. He then joined the Marine Corps. She told me that when he returned home from overseas, he was not the same person anymore. She said his personality changed drastically and his behavior was noticeably different. He became more distant. At the time, it all sounded like some bullshit ass excuse to me and I still hated him. I was getting a little older then, and I remember telling myself, *When I have kids, I'm always going to be there for them no matter what the situation is.* There is no way in hell I was gonna repeat that cycle. I wouldn't have cared if my dad was broke, blind, crippled, or crazy—I just wanted him to be around.

There were rumors of him having post-traumatic stress disorder (PTSD) or some other kind of mental health issue, but I had no knowledge of any of that at the time. Now that I'm an adult, I honestly feel that mental health played a huge role in him not being in any of his children's lives and I have no ill feelings towards him. Overall, he's still a cool guy. Therefore, I appreciate you, Herman Jones.

CHAPTER 2

Premature Fatherhood

I realized early that my future kids would never feel the same way about me and how important it was for me to be active in their lives. I'm an only child and I knew I would have more than one child. I was never able to experience a sibling relationship. I'd always hear stories from my other bestfriend Mike about how annoying his little sisters were, or I'd see the big-brother-li'l-brother relationship between Jermaine and Derrick. Jamar, my other bestfriend, had two older sisters and Adrienne was the youngest. He'd always act as the man of the house. He didn't take no shit when it came to his sisters. Jamar would literally shoot somebody if necessary to protect his sisters. He also made sure none of the homies tried to get with Adrienne.

Subconsciously, I believe these experiences helped to shape my views on parenthood. I knew from a very young age that I would have kids early, and I always pictured in my mind what kind of father I wanted to be. My journey to fatherhood began a little after I dropped out of California

State University Northridge (CSUN) in 1999. I was working at a telemarketing company in Chatsworth, California, selling ink cartridges. One day at work, a coworker of mine, Erin, walked in with this cute, little, light-skinned, Pocahontas-lookin' chick, and I was like, "Damn. Who is that!?" I turned my head and pretended I didn't see her because all the other guys were checking her out also. I eventually found out that she was a new hire, and I thought to myself, *OK, I gotta see what's up with that.*

A couple days later, I was able to get a closer look and realized she was the same girl I used to see on CSUN's campus from time to time. During our lunch break, we all met outside at the food truck and that's when I met Qiana. We immediately connected and I had a sharp sense that something special was brewing. Qiana was an "around the way" girl for sure, always laughing, down to earth, and with a reckless mouth. Not surprised because she went to one of the roughest high schools in LA: Dorsey High. From her looks, you'd think she went to Westchester High where I attended or Hamilton, but nah, Qiana was a li'l hood and I loved that about her. I loved how she always put on this tough exterior but I always saw through it and appreciated her more sensitive, caring side.

We were a power couple for sure. We did everything together and rarely got into arguments, being that we were only twenty-two, twenty-three years old. Now that I'm a grown man, looking back, we were babies still, not realizing that life was just beginning. Qiana and I spent so much time together that it was inevitable that I got the "we need to talk" call.

When Qiana told me she was pregnant I was like, *Whoooa!*, with a happy feeling inside but afraid to show it in the moment because I didn't know how she felt about it yet. We both agreed to become parents, and that decision was the best feeling ever because now I get to be the father I never had and also the father I always wanted to be. The entire pregnancy process was amazing to me, from getting the first ultrasound where you can hear the baby's heart beating, to seeing the full fetus where you can actually feel and see the baby's movements. I'll never forget the excitement I felt knowing that fatherhood was just months away.

March 1, 2001 is when Qiana and I introduced Jahad to the world. Jahad was a healthy baby—silly and full of joy. He was a happy baby, and he always kept a smile on his face. He also kept my ass up in the middle of the night regularly and that wasn't fun at all. *LOL*. Months later, my relationship with Qiana began to change. The details are a little fuzzy, but I'm sure it had a lot to do with us being young and me not being mature enough to keep the relationship strong. Qiana and I eventually ended our relationship. She moved out and this is where my experience with coparenting began.

In the beginning, it was tough because I didn't have a car at the time and I depended on Qiana to drop off Jahad and pick him up on the weekends. She would keep him during the week for some months until I was finally able to get a car. During that time, I would help with food and clothes to help ease the load. We then agreed to a 50-50 joint custody schedule where I would take him to school and pick him up two days out of the week and we would rotate weekends. We split daycare fees and we both provided health insurance for him. There were times when I was in between jobs and was not able to contribute as much financially. During this time, I was introduced to family court.

Qiana filed a motion for child support. I remember this is when I lost all respect for Qiana. I felt betrayed because in my mind I felt like she knew how much I was trying to get back on my feet. She knew I had one strike on my record, which made me a felon and made it very difficult for me to find a decent job. However, this was what I was feeling at the time, and I had no idea what she was feeling or what was going through her mind. I'm sure her feelings and reasoning were valid at that moment. We went to one court hearing, and months later Qiana dropped the child support order. A few years later, I asked her why she decided to drop the child support and she said her boyfriend at the the time convinced her to. Salute to that brotha. *LOL*. I appreciate cha'.

Ultimately, we managed to successfully stick to a 50-50 schedule up until Jahad turned seventeen. Sixteen years straight with no gaps in between. Although Qiana and I had a bumpy start, we were mature enough to realize that it's important to put Jahad's needs first. We were mature enough to understand the importance of Jahad having both parents consistent in his life despite our differences. We were both raised without our fathers and I'm grateful that we had matured enough to break the cycle. To this day, Qiana and I are good friends and I will always have love for her. I truly appreciate you, Qiana. Thank you.

CHAPTER 3

◀ Red Flags ▶

I'm now around twenty-five years old, a single father facing the challenges of supporting and raising a child on my own. I struggled trying to find consistent work because at eighteen years old, I was caught for a felony for doing some dumb shit in my freshman year in college. I was sentenced to one year in the Los Angeles County Jail, however I was out of there in six months. The cost of living in LA was kicking my ass. I was paying rent, bills, car notes, etc. on my own. It wasn't always sweet, but I can definitely say I made the best out of what I had.

I believe it was the summer of 2003 when one of my close friends, John, invited me to a house party. This was no average house party. This was the ultimate mansion house party in Malibu, California. John had a friend whose parents lived in Malibu, and his parents were out of town for the weekend. So they decided to throw the party of the summer. John asked me to invite some friends from Inglewood and LA, specifically female friends, and I was like, *Cool*. At the time, I really didn't have many female friends so I reached out to a couple of close friends and asked them to invite some females. I ended up driving with my homie Malcolm, and the other homies were gonna meet us up there.

As usual, we first stopped at the liquor store so that we could have a nice, lil buzz when we pull up to Malibu. Christian Brothers was my choice of drink at the time because it was cheap and it got me right. We pulled up to the house, and I immediately knew it was was gonna be a poppin' night. It was a three-story house, and the second level was made of glass so you can see directly in the house. There were people everywhere. As we made our way in, I immediately smelled the potency of marijuana in the air. The music was loud, and you would think you were in a rapper's crib. I had never been in a house this size and especially in Malibu.

I made my way to the kitchen and there were bottles of liquor, wine, and champagne everywhere. The girls were all super good-looking and I'm thinking to myself, *I'm bangin' something tonight. LOL.* I noticed how most of the girls were all super friendly and full of smiles. A guy came up to me and said, "Yo, bro, I got the ecstasy pills on the deck." I was like, "Aight, cool. But I don't do ecstasy. I'm good with my Christian Brothers." A few minutes later, my homie Malcolm said one of the girls he invited was outside parking, and he asked me to walk outside with him to get them. I was like, "OK, cool. Let's go."

We made our way outside and from a distance I noticed the girl in the bright red pants. As we got closer, she began to look a lil cute but I wasn't sure if it was them or not because there were so many people outside walking towards the house. We walked up to the white car and Malcolm gave the girl in the red pants a hug. He introduced me to her and in my head I was thinking, *Yeah, I like you already.* "I'm Kenyada. Nice to meet you, Denise." We worked our way back to the party and I immediately pulled Malcolm to the side and asked, "Thats you, my nigga?" Malcolm gave me a big ass smile and said, "I'm trying to see what's up." So I asked again, "Na, nigga. Is that you? You hittin' that?" He said no and that he recently met her at gym class at CSUN. I was like, "Cool. She wide open then."

At this point, everyone was now enjoying the party, dancing, smoking, popping pills, and having a good time. I didn't move around the house much because I wanted to make sure no other guy took a shot at Denise. I kept her within arm's reach. We hit it off pretty good and at some point, I didn't see her as somebody I just wanted to bang for the night. She gave me a different vibe. I knew she was different. I knew she wasn't that type, and as the night went on, I drew more interest in her. The party was coming to an end so I asked Denise for her phone number and told her I'd be hitting her up soon.

A couple days later, I gave her a call during my lunch break. She answered and we talked for a few minutes. During the conversation, I could tell that Denise was a good girl. She was definitely a "valley girl" as us city boys would say. Valley girls were the girls who were raised outside the city of LA. These were the girls that the city boys would take advantage of because we felt they had no sense of how we operated in the city. We assumed valley girls were somewhat airheads and were super easy to get with.

However, Denise was different. She was very quiet, chill, and easy to talk to to. We talked on the phone a couple more days, and then I invited her to come hang out and chill at my place. She came over, we talked more, and this is when I learned her parents had been divorced for a few years. She explained that her mom remarried and that she was living with her stepdad and two brothers. I learned that her stepdad owned a business just blocks away from my apartment. Denise, her mother, and her older brother all worked for his business. I thought to myself, *This girl got it made. She's privileged.* We talked about other things, and I could tell that Denise and I were really feeling each other.

We continued to talk and hang out almost every day to the point where she damn near moved in with me. It even got to a point where Denise's mother would be upset with her for hanging out with me a lot. I remember there were times when Denise's mom would call her and make her go home because she was with me so much. A few weeks later, Denise eventually met Jahad. Jahad was about nine or ten months old at that point. Denise instantly befriended Jahad and from there I was even more interested in her. Jahad liked Denise and the two of them developed a cool lil bond, and I sincerely believed Denise cared about him.

After a few months of hanging out, we decided it was time for me to meet her family. I believe it was Thanksgiving

Day when I met her family. Denise's mom is a white woman, and I had never been around a white woman before. So, at first, I felt a little awkward, but soon enough I settled in. Everyone seemed pretty cool and down to earth. I would just be watching the football game and then all of a sudden, Denise's mom brings out the old family photos. I was definitely interested in seeing the photos so I could have some good laughs. While flipping through the photo album, something immediately caught my attention. I noticed that Denise's mom cut out all the pictures that Denise's real dad were in. I thought to myself, *Wow, that's crazy. Why would she do that?* I paid it no mind but definitely took a mental note. Thanksgiving ended up being fun, and I had a really good time with her family. By then, it was safe to say Denise and I were officially a couple.

The following month, Denise invited Jahad and me to spend Christmas with her family. Qiana and I agreed that Jahad would spend the day with her and her family and I would have him in the evening, so that worked out perfectly. We made it to Denise's house and as I walked in, there was a huge Christmas tree with hundreds of gifts under it. I thought, *Damn. They rich rich.* I've never seen anything like that except on TV. So as we worked our way to the living room, there were these huge Christmas stockings filled with all kinds of things, from gift cards to candy, and two of them had my name and Jahad's name on them. I was blown away but I played it cool inside. Denise's family welcomed Jahad with open arms and that was a good first impression to me.

They surprised me and Jahad with a lot of gifts, and I can honestly say I was not expecting anything.

Denise's mom took an extra special liking to Jahad, and they also developed a good bond. Her family treated Jahad as if he was really a part of their family. I admired that about them. Opening gifts was fun, but in my mind I was thinking these were way too many gifts to be given to her seventeen-year-old and twenty-seven-year old sons. I started to feel like she was buying their loyalty or something, but I couldn't quite put a finger on it. It just seemed a bit too much. But, then again, this was new to me, not them, so I paid it no mind but definitely took a mental note. So, boom! Now we're a full-fledged couple and life is great.

Denise's mom and stepdad would attend all of Jahad's basketball games, and they would babysit him from time to time so that Denise and I could go out. Denise's stepdad was in his late forties, Middle Eastern, had a heavy accent, and had no biological children of his own, so he enjoyed playing with Jahad. I was cool with that. There's this stereotype that Middle Eastern men are controlling patriarchs, but I didn't get that vibe from him.

By now, a year or two had passed and our relationship was in great shape. I was working; Denise was in school and still working at her stepdad's business. Denise started expressing frustration with working for the business because she'd been working there a few years and did not a receive a raise. She felt as though she was taking on more tasks than what her job title required so she was ready to leave the business. I encouraged her to apply to other companies. I figured at least she can explore her options and this would give her a better idea of what she's really worth. She really wanted to apply out, but she was afraid that her mom would be upset. She was afraid to disappoint her mom and stepdad so she stayed the course. She felt she owed it to them because they were paying her college tuition and covering most of her living expenses.

I never understood why she was so afraid to venture out. In my mind, I felt like her stepdad's business was pretty stable and it would always be there if all else failed. I felt like her mom and stepdad would understand and support her in trying something different. I was wrong. I also remember asking Denise about her mother's side of the family because she never mentioned them. She always talked about her biological dad's family. Denise mentioned that her mother's mom and dad disowned her mom because she had a child/children with a black man. Denise mentioned they had little to no contact with them. I thought that was pretty fucked up, but it didn't surprise me one bit. I paid it no mind but definitely took mental notes.

At this point, Denise is pretty much living with me. She would bring clothes to stay the night and leave for work in the morning. From my place, it took literally four to five minutes to get there as opposed to forty-five minutes from her mom's place. One morning, Denise was feeling sick and I remember her rushing to the bathroom. She was throwing up as if she had been food-poisoned or something, and it was pretty bad. She forced herself to go to work but ended up leaving because she felt miserable. She felt sick for a couple days. It then led us to believe that maybe she was pregnant. In fact, she was.

Once the pregnancy was official, I became super excited. I was so happy to know that I would be having a second child. I felt like this time I would have the girl I've always dreamed of. However, I noticed I was the only one excited. Denise was more worried rather than excited. We talked about the pregnancy, and she was very worried about what her mother would think. She was afraid that her mother would be disappointed in her. Denise then explained to me that if we were to have a child, her mother would kick her out of the house, stop paying her college tuition, and cut her off financially. In the moment, I understood why her mother would feel that way being that Denise was still young and in college. But I tried to explain to her that once the baby arrived, her mother would change and be more supportive. Denise wasn't hearing all that. I started to feel a way about it. I could not believe what I was hearing while at the same time, I respected Denise's feelings.

In my mind, I thought, *How in the hell are we gonna let her mother decide whether we have a child or not?* I also thought, *What kind of mother would do such a thing?* So now, at this point, all the mental notes I took early on were starting to make sense. I started to reflect on the family photos where Denise's mom cut out her father's pictures, the times her mother would make her go home because she was spending too much time with me, how her mom would spoil and over-compensate them, etc. At that point, it became clear to me that her mother was the matriarch of the family, with full control of their lives. It became clear that her spoiling them so much was her way to control and accrue their loyalty.

After further discussion, Denise felt it was best to terminate the pregnancy out of fear that her mother would disown her the same way her grandparents did her mom. There were other small factors, but the ultimate decision was based on fear. I remember feeling like shit for months. I was sad and upset, and I quickly started to dislike her mother. Denise never knew I developed these feelings. I always kept them to myself and acted as if everything was normal. I had been taking care of myself since I was eighteen years old so this type of situation was new to me. I never knew a parent could have so much control over their child to the point where the child would sacrifice their own happiness out of fear of being disowned or judged by that parent. It made no sense to me, however, I decided to stay in the relationship because I still loved and cared about Denise. Then a year passed and things went back to normal.

CHAPTER 4

Déjà Vu

E arly one morning before work, Denise started having morning sickness and throwing up again. *Yep! She's pregnant!* 👤 I thought, *Here we go again.* This time I wasn't excited because I was unsure of what we were going to decide. I started to revisit the same feelings I had the previous year and I didn't like that at all. I was not looking forward to having the conversation again, but obviously it had to be done. As we talked, I could feel the energy was different. It was a short conversation, and Denise said she wanted to have the baby. I was fucking ecstatic! This was the moment where my dreams were coming into fruition. I was finally going to have two children, and Jahad will not be the only child like I was. I could finally experience the ups and downs of a sibling relationship. This was one of the best feelings in my life.

But I was also afraid for Denise because she had to break the news to her mom. I was afraid of what the consequences would be for her. She was also afraid but soon mustered the strength to tell her mom. As we expected, her mother didn't take it too well. I wasn't there when she broke the news, and the details were kinda fuzzy during this particular moment. But it's safe to say that after a couple weeks, her mom and family were on board. Boom! So now the stage is set. Time to begin the longest nine-month process of my life. The entire process was amazing, from the doctor visits to the changed eating habits, stomach growth, and name dropping. There was no doubt that I wanted a baby girl. In my mind, it just had to be a girl to make it complete. I had been envisioning having a girl since high school. I had always envisioned how our relationship would be. I envisioned being the cool dad, and I just knew we would be like best friends. That feeling is giving me the chills right now as I'm writing this.

A couple months have passed, and it was time for the ultrasound visit where we were going to find out the gender of the baby. I'll never forget the nurse rubbing the gel on Denise's stomach and the moment of anticipation. Hands sweaty, heart jumping out of my chest, and nervous as all hell. Finally, the gender was revealed. It's a girl! Did you read what I just wrote!? It's a girl! It's safe to say I was the happiest man living at that moment. I couldn't wait to let Jahad know he was going to be a big brother. He was only four years old at the time, but I still couldn't wait to tell him.

Months passed and it was time for me meet to my baby girl for the first time. The year was 2005, and it was August 25th when Denise's water broke. It was around 9:30 p.m., and I was in the living room watching the news as this is also the time Hurricane Katrina invaded New Orleans. Remember, I'm from New Orleans and ninety percent of my family lived there during this time. This was a bittersweet time in my life. I was juggling the emotions of having a child and the emotions of watching this natural disaster attempt to wipe out my people.

As we were headed to the hospital, I was constantly on the phone with my mom and cousins, getting updates. Beau, my mother's husband, decided to stay at their house in New Orleans because he felt he's survived enough hurricanes in his lifetime already. A lot of people felt that way in New Orleans but also a good bit of people decided to evacuate. My mother's home was struck hard, and Beau ended up on the roof of the house as the flood rose at a rapid speed. Luckily, there were plenty of neighbors around to help everyone get safely to the roof. Eventually, they were all rescued.

Meanwhile, we were checked in at Cedars-Sinai Medical Center and Denise's contractions were getting stronger and stronger. The pain was too much for Denise so she decided to get an epidural shot for relief. We were now just playing the waiting game and, all of a sudden, I got a phone call from my uncle Ahmad. Ahmad told me he was on the rooftop of a hospital and he had been stuck with some other people for hours. He also told me that my other uncle, his brother Mjiri, evacuated to the New Orleans Superdome. While at the hospital, I was hearing all the nasty stories about what was happening in the dome and I was hoping Mjiri was safe. My uncle was pretty solid, so in my mind, I knew he was holding his own, but the worry was still there. Fortunately, everyone in my family survived Katrina while, unfortunately, most of their homes suffered severe damage.

I was still at the hospital, trying to soak all this in while being there to support Denise. Then the nurse walked in the room to explain to us that they were going to induce labor. I could feel it getting closer and closer to delivery. I became more antsy and excited at the time. It was August 27th, 2005, at around five or six in the morning. The doctor came in the room and said, "It's time to deliver a baby." Denise was feeling the pressure from the contractions. The doctors were telling her to take deep breaths and to push as hard as she could. Continue to take deep breaths and push, push, push. I glanced down and saw the baby's head slowly making its way out. Then, immediately, I started to feel lightheaded. *Oh shit! I think Imma pass out!* was how I felt. The nurse quickly gave me a cup of ice chips to chew on. They said it would help ease the feeling.

I had to get away for a second, and I began to pace back and forth to gather myself. The damn ice chips ain't working. I was about to pass the fuck out. Eventually, I gathered myself and headed back over to Denise. In a matter of seconds, the baby was out. Just that quick. The nurse handed me the scissors to cut the umbilical cord and just like that my vision became my reality. On August 27, 2005, Isis Jones was born, weighing 9 lbs (and I can't remember the ounces). Isis was very pale with long feet that had extra soft skin hanging from her big toes. Her hair was dark and curly. She had big, chubby cheeks that I loved to bite on. I'll never forget that moment. Both Denise and Isis's vital signs were clear. They were both healthy and it was time to take Isis home to meet her big brother Jahad and her new family.

CHAPTER 5

The Calm Before the Storm

We moved into a two-bedroom apartment in Van Nuys. Our first official place together. The area wasn't the greatest, but it was all we could afford at the time. We began our journey as a family and the first couple of years were great. I continued to share 50-50 custody with Jahad, and he always got excited when he came to our place because he couldn't wait to see Isis. Isis was around three or four at this point, and it was time for her to leave the home daycare provider and enroll in a school. We also wanted to move to a better area, but we couldn't afford it. Denise's parents offered to pay Isis's tuition. This was a big deal because it put us in a position to be able to move. We then moved to a better area in Northridge, minutes from Denise's stepdad's business and Isis's new school. Denise was also able to continue going to school at CSUN, so everything worked out perfectly.

On the weekends, when Jahad would be with Qiana, Isis would occasionally stay the weekend with Denise's parents so that she and I could have some time together. Slowly, Denise's parents wanted to keep Isis every weekend, and this is when things started to go left. Denise had no issue with Isis going there every weekend, but I did. I was okay with it occasionally, but they wanted it to be a routine. That would be taking away time from Jahad and me, and I didn't think that was cool at all. I guess Denise felt obligated to allow Isis to go because, after all, her parents were paying Isis's tuition and they had just co-signed for Denise to get a new car. This did not sit well with me.

I was very appreciative of her parents for volunteering to help us get into a better situation, but I felt like that gave them no right to have Isis every weekend in return. I struggled with that for a while and I started to feel trapped. Denise's parents would also spoil Isis, which is common for grandparents to do, but this was a bit extreme to me. I started to feel like Denise's mom was trying to gain control of Isis the same way she controlled Denise and her brothers. Denise's stepdad has no biological children of his own and I'm sure that played a role in them wanting to spend a lot of time with Isis. It gave them the feeling of what it's like to have their own child.

I felt like, out of respect for me, they should have known where to draw the line. I don't believe any active parent would agree with that kind of arrangement. For a while, I struggled with how to have this conversation with Denise because I didn't want to come off the wrong way. During this time, my great-grandmother passed away. I planned to fly to New Orleans for the funeral by myself because I couldn't afford a plane ticket for all four of us. Denise then suggested she would talk to her mother about buying plane tickets for her and Isis using her stepdad's business credit card. They had frequent flying miles and usually never pay for flights. Denise then said her mom agreed to purchase our tickets, but the only issue was there was not enough to pay for Jahad's ticket. I thought to myself, *That's bullshit.* But at the same time, what can I say?

I felt that was a smack in the face because I knew they could afford plane tickets for all of us. Why wouldn't they get a ticket for him too being that they had a good relationship with him? I felt like I'd just rather go alone, but at the same time, this would be an opportunity for Isis to meet my family for the first time. I kept the anger to myself and decided to go without Jahad. I felt bad about leaving him behind. I started to build more animosity towards Denise's mom and also began to feel angry with Denise.

Our trip to New Orleans was good, but when we returned, things continued to go left. I noticed Denise's relationship with Jahad started to sway. There would be times when Jahad wanted to push Isis in her stroller while at the mall or just when we were out in general and Denise wouldn't let him. I remember Jahad wanting to feed Isis sometimes and she wouldn't let him. I started to witness her attitude towards Jahad changing, and I just couldn't figure out why. I was taking mental notes while at the same time giving myself time to make sure I was really seeing what I was seeing.

When Jahad was away with Qiana, I started to notice that Denise appeared to be happier. When he was with us, her mood switched. I'll never forget the day I needed to make a quick run to pick up some groceries for dinner and Jahad frantically ran behind me, asking me to take him with me. Jahad has never had an issue with staying with Denise if I needed to leave. The look on his face concerned me, but I trusted he'd be okay until I got back. When I returned, Jahad was sitting in the living room with a look of excitement when he saw me. I was like, *Hmmm, this is very strange.* Now my full attention was on, and my thoughts were all over the place.

A few weeks went by, and it became clear to me that Denise had no interest in continuing her relationship with Jahad. I began to feel stuck in the middle of having to choose between my son and my girlfriend. Horrible feeling. I didn't know how to express my feelings to her, nor did I have anyone to talk to about what was happening. In my mind, I knew things were about to get bad. I felt it. On the weekends, when Jahad and Isis were away, I started to hang out with my friends more than with Denise. I started drinking more and staying out late. My emotions were running wild, and I didn't wanna be around her anymore. I needed to escape and get away from all the confusion and tension that was building. I'm sure she noticed the change in my behavior, but we never discussed it. We continued our day-to-day relationship, but I'm sure we both felt something was wrong. We ignored it and pretended everything was okay. Well, at least, in my mind we did.

I eventually called Denise while she was working and told her that we needed to talk later that night. In the conversation, I explained to her how I noticed her relationship with Jahad had drastically changed. I gave examples and explained to her what I've been seeing. I explained to her that Jahad was not comfortable with being around her anymore and how that made me feel. Her response was she didn't notice any change. She felt as though things were still normal and that she still cared for Jahad. She said she would try to be more aware of her actions and that she would never want us to feel that way towards her. I felt good after our talk. I felt like it released a ton of weight from my shoulders. I was excited to see things change and get back to normal.

For a couple months, things actually got back to normal. I noticed Denise attempting to be friendlier with Jahad but it seemed forced, not natural like before. While their relationship tried to get back on track, I still hadn't fully addressed my issue with Isis going to her parents' house every weekend. I thought maybe I should give it a little more time since we were already dealing with the Jahad issue. Another year of Christmas approached, and this time, Jahad spent Christmas with Qiana. Qiana dropped him off the following day. Jahad had a bag of gifts for Isis. At that time, Qiana and I were still having small issues related to things that happened in the past, so I was surprised she would send gifts for Isis. She brought some nice clothes for Isis. I took that as a peace offering. I felt like this was Qiana's way of ending our feud without actually saying it, and from there, Qiana and I remained cordial.

It meant a lot to me. I never would've thought Qiana and I would be at peace. However, Denise was not impressed. I made sure I remembered the clothes Qiana brought for Isis to see how Denise would feel when I dressed Isis or if she would dress Isis in the clothes. I knew Denise was aware of the clothes Qiana brought but she never dressed Isis in the clothes. I took that as a smack in the face because Denise was there to witness all the feuds I had with Qiana. I expected Denise to also accept Qiana's peace offering and at least allow Isis to wear the clothes. She didn't. Now I have another issue with Denise. I was now dealing with three issues at once: Isis going to her grandparents' house every weekend, Denise's behavior towards Jahad, and now Denise's attitude towards Qiana.

Back to the Jahad situation. As I stated earlier, Denise tried to reconcile her relationship with him but that was short-lived. I remember Googling some information to try and help me understand her behavioral change. I came across postpartum depression. I read several articles and some explained separation anxiety where, after a new mother gives birth, it's common for her to feel like she needs space from people around her—something to that degree. The articles helped me understand the different types of postpartum but, most importantly, convinced me that it's a real thing. I remember bringing this information to Denise because I felt like it was a strong possibility that it was what was happening to her. In my heart, I felt like postpartum depression was the cause of her changing behavior towards Jahad. I felt like I could work through it and that there was hope in getting some help to fix our situation.

Unfortunately, Denise denied even considering postpartum depression. She looked at me like I was crazy and had no interest in what I was saying. I felt like I did all the right things by communicating all my concerns to her, but in the end, all my concerns were dismissed. That made me feel like shit. At that point, I began to emotionally check out of the relationship. My heart was broken because I could never imagine anything like this happening. I was confused but my intuition was telling me that the relationship was over, and I agreed. I started hanging out on the weekends again. I started partying more, going to more get-togethers, hanging out with my single friends, and even reaching out to girls I dated before I met Denise. I would come home at two or three in the morning regularly. There were times when I'd be getting text messages in the middle of the night, and I'm sure Denise noticed.

I'll never forget the day Denise was riding with me to Lens Crafters by the Northridge Mall because I needed to pick up my contact lenses. I accidentally left my phone in the car where the screen was visible. As I returned to my car, my phone was ringing and it clearly said "Vanessa" on the screen. I knew Denise saw the screen, but she pretended she didn't and didn't say anything about it. Denise knew the names of my female friends, and Vanessa was not any of my female friends' names. I remember not caring whether Denise would say something or not. In my mind, I felt as though Denise didn't give a fuck about me or my feelings, so why the fuck should I care about hers at that point? I was angry for sure.

Vanessa was this bad Latino chick I met during one of my nights out. She was also in a relationship. Her relationship was not going well either so we both had something in common. It was easy to communicate with Vanessa because we both knew what our boundaries were, and we did not want to get each other in trouble with our significant others while we were both dealing with our relationship issues. Vanessa and I made time to hang out, and it quickly turned into a sexual relationship. The irony was that Vanessa's issues with her boyfriend stemmed from him hanging out with his friends all night, partying. She felt like he wasn't giving her enough time and attention. Therefore, she came to the conclusion that he was out cheating on her.

Prior to my issues with Denise, I was one hundred percent committed and faithful to our relationship. When I explained to Vanessa what was happening within my relationship, she took a liking to the fact that I was committed. She quickly started having feelings for me, which led to her breaking all the communication rules we had agreed on. I eventually cut ties with her because I knew I wasn't ready to be in a new relationship, especially when I was already in one. I didn't feel any guilt for my actions. All I knew was I was hurt, confused, and angry, and I didn't understand why the girl I was in love with all of a sudden neglected my son. I don't know why I channeled my behavior in that direction; it just happened. I began to see my vision of us being one big, happy family quickly turning into a nightmare. I was put in a situation where I had to choose either Jahad or her. There was no in between. There was no way I could balance the two while we were all under the same roof. Who would you choose?

CHAPTER 6

Hell Hath No Fury Like a Woman Scorned (The Pre-Birth of Parental Alienation)

I made my decision, but I needed time to process my thoughts and to mentally prepare for what was about to happen. A couple weeks had passed and the energy in our home was very low. One night, before us going to bed, I decided to have a talk with Denise. I explained to her that I needed some space. I explained to her how confused, hurt, and angry I felt. It was one of the toughest conversations I've ever had to have. I could've never imagined those words ever coming out of my mouth. I loved her, she was my best friend, but I knew I was making the right decision. I explained to her that I didn't want to end the relationship but we should separate instead until we could figure out how to repair it. It was a sad and emotional conversation.

We ultimately agreed to separate. I was able to find a one-bedroom apartment in Encino, while Denise moved back to Valencia to live with her parents. A one-bedroom apartment was all I could afford. I made it so Jahad and Isis could share the bedroom and I'd make the living room my bedroom. They had bunk beds, and the room was a decent size. The transition was pretty smooth in the beginning. Denise and I were on good terms. We agreed that Isis could spend time with me every other weekend until she was able to find herself a place closer in the valley. After a few months, Denise was able to find a place in Sherman Oaks. Her apartment was literally fifteen minutes away from mine and about twenty-five minutes away from her stepdad's business.

During our separation, we remained in close contact with each other. We went out to dinner several times, and I even spent Christmas with her and her family at that time. Now that we were living only fifteen minutes apart, we agreed that Isis can have overnight stays at my place on Tuesdays in addition to every other weekend. At the time, my schedule with Jahad was Mondays, Tuesdays, and every other weekend. This way, Jahad and I could spend more time with Isis. We agreed to slowly transition Isis to the same schedule as Jahad's. I started picking Isis up from daycare, but I always got there just minutes before they closed at 6 p.m. Everyone knows it can take up to two hours to get from the city to the valley, and usually Isis was always the last to get picked up. Fortunately, Denise had the luxury of working for her stepdad, so sometimes she would get Isis early and I would just pick her up from their family business.

The arrangement worked really well. I'd make sure Isis completed her homework, and I'd also sign off on her reading logs. It was extra special to see Jahad and Isis doing their homework at the same time. I'd peek in the room and there were times when Jahad would help Isis with putting her vocabulary words into sentences. I loved seeing that. I even took some pictures while they weren't looking. Aside from talking about Isis, communication between me and Denise began to slow down. The only time we talked was to discuss pick-up or drop-off arrangements.

A few months passed by, so I decided to ask Denise out to dinner. At dinner, we were pretty much informing each other about where we were in our lives. Denise mentioned she went on a couple of dates, and I also explained how I did the same. It was an awkward moment for me, but I was glad we were able to talk about it. I still had feelings for her and I could feel the jealousy in my heart, but I played it cool. We eventually grew apart as time passed, and we decided to end the relationship. And so my story begins here.

A couple of months after our break-up, I called Denise to inform her that the open enrollment would begin in a few months and that I'd be removing her from my health benefits. I explained that Jahad and Isis would remain, and she had a few months to get on a plan through their family business. She explained how the monthly premiums were too expensive through her employer and that she couldn't afford it. She explained that she felt I should keep her on my benefits as a type of compensation to her since she had more time with Isis. Denise got upset as if I was doing something wrong.

I didn't understand why she felt it was my responsibility to keep her on my benefits when we were no longer in a relationship. I could sense she felt as if I was punishing her or something to that effect, but that wasn't the case. Also, during our conversation, I explained to her how I felt that it was time to increase my parenting time with Isis. I proposed every Tuesday and Thursday, and every other weekend. I could sense she was uneasy about the conversation, but I didn't understand why. We had already agreed to increase my parenting time once they were settled in the new place, and it had been three or four months already. I sensed she was upset about me removing her from my benefits, but I felt like it was the right thing to do now that we've moved on.

I knew Denise would be okay financially because her parents were also providing financial support to her and Isis. I knew there was no way her parents would let her struggle. She said she needed a couple days to think about it, and I was okay with that. A couple days had passed so I followed up with her to get an update, and she agreed to my proposal. We agreed to a 50-50 custody arrangement, and I was super excited because I could to spend more time with Isis now. I was even more excited because I was able to change my schedule with Qiana to have the same schedule as Isis. Isis was okay with it and didn't show any resistance or worry. Denise and I honored this schedule for a few months without any issues.

Months later, I received a call from Denise, explaining to me that she had enrolled Isis in piano class. I had no problem with Isis being enrolled in piano class, but her piano lessons were on Thursdays which was my custodial day. Piano class was from 6 p.m. to 7:15 p.m. in North Hollywood. There was no way I could make in time to take Isis to class since I was driving from LA to the valley and dealing with traffic. I asked Denise if she could change the piano class schedule to one of her custodial days, and she said it was only offered on Thursdays. I was pissed because I felt she was lying and it was wrong for her to schedule an activity on our agreed custody day without talking to me about it first. It was more than an inconvenience to me and a waste of custodial time with Isis.

To get to North Hollywood from LA on a Thursday, I'd arrive at the end of piano class. Then, we would get back home at around 8:30 p.m. Then she'd need to eat dinner, do her homework, shower, and be in bed by 9:30. It made no sense. I disagreed but Denise took it upon herself to pick up Isis before I could get to daycare to bring Isis to piano class. I was super pissed! So I called Denise to explain that it wasn't okay, but her argument was, "Why don't you want Isis to attend piano lessons?" I had no problem with Isis going to piano class. My problem was Isis attending on my custodial day in addition to causing an inconvenience to my commute.

Denise and I had our very first argument ever. At the end of the conversation, I calmed down and suggested we get help from a professional. The only thing I could think of was to go to family court to see if there were counselors or someone who could help parents with our situation. I suggested we go the following day. I was willing to call out sick from work, but she said she couldn't make it the following day and we should go the day after instead. I said, "Cool. No problem." The very next day, Jahad and I were at home eating dinner when I heard a knock on my door. I answered the door and it was Denise's younger brother serving me court papers. I was shocked and at a loss for words. Her brother and I were always really cool with each other. I liked him a lot and I couldn't believe he would even agree to this. I immediately felt betrayed by Denise and her brother.

After reading a couple of lines on the paperwork, my heart started to palpitate. I began breathing heavily, and my hand was shaking so much to point where I couldn't read the words anymore. I threw the papers on my bed, sat for a few minutes, and stared into space. My food had gotten cold and I completely lost my appetite. I thought, *Why did she lie? Why did she do this?* She told me the day before that she wouldn't be able to go, but she went anyway. At that point, I knew this would end up being a nightmare. I spent the next couple of days thinking about what to do next. I received a letter in the mail from Denise's attorney, stating that she would be representing her in court. I thought, *Wow, this is really happening.* I had lost all respect for Denise. The letter also came with a mediation date and time to speak with a counselor before the actual court date.

On our very first mediation, Denise showed up with her mother. Denise couldn't look me in the eye, but her mother had no problem giving me the mean mug. She looked at me as if I was being arraigned for physically abusing her daughter or something to that effect. It was a cold look as if she was trying to tell me they were about to lock me up and throw away the key. I could feel her animosity for me through her eyes. All I could do was laugh and shake my head from within, thinkin' to myself, *What could she have possibly told her family about me to make them all of a sudden see me in a different way?*

During mediation, no one is allowed in the room so her mother had to wait outside. Denise went on to explain to the counselor that Isis would rather attend piano class than spend her time with me. She continued to explain how Isis would get sad at the thought of not going to piano class. The counselor was no help at all. She immediately showed favor to Denise's explanation. Denise was soft-spoken; she spoke as if Isis was distraught and or in some kind of danger when she was with me. This was my very first time in life experiencing someone that I considered a friend, girlfriend, and person I truly loved speak so bad about my character. I sat there in disbelief. I couldn't believe all the bullshit coming out her mouth. During our mediation of almost an hour, we were not able to agree to continue our 50-50 custody agreement. The mediator explained that we would need to see a judge and that it usually would take two to three months. Denise went her way and I went mine. Isis was six years old during this time, and I was not financially prepared to retain a lawyer.

Since the split, I made sure to document everything. I saved daycare receipts, clothing receipts, copies of Isis's homework assignments, prescription receipts, EVERYTHING! I felt I didn't need to hire an attorney because in my heart, I knew I was supporting my children. I knew I was no deadbeat dad. That could never be me. I couldn't understand why Denise had such a problem with us sharing our time with Isis, especially when we lived so close in distance. I was always consistent with picking her up and dropping her off at school. Always consistent with providing food, shelter, and a safe living environment for her. I was always consistent in taking the kids to the park, swimming pools, and theme parks on my weekends. I was always consistent in teaching the kids to have good morals and how to treat people with respect.

Jahad, Isis, and I had a strong bond. I loved being with them and watching them grow. I love Isis just as much as Denise does. I felt it was best to represent myself in court despite Denise's parents hiring an expensive Beverly Hills attorney for her. I felt as though any judge in America would be able to see that I was a responsible father and on top of that, I had receipts! I had no fear facing a judge as I felt the truth would set me free. I had no prior knowledge about the family court system, and I was very confident with my presentation.

During the three-month waiting period for our first official court date, we started to have issues with the custody exchanges. I noticed how Isis's behavior started to change when I picked her up from Denise's family business. All of a sudden, she appeared to be unhappy to see me. She displayed this behavior for a few weeks, and then it went from her being unhappy to crying when I arrived to pick her up. I was totally confused as to why she was reacting this way. She would refuse to get in the car with me. Isis's mom and family would be there, encouraging her to leave with me. Her mom would hold her and say things like, "It's okay. You'll be alright. If you need me, just call me. I'm here for you. Don't cry. It's okay to go with him."

I'd get so frustrated deep inside, thinking to myself, *What the fuck are they telling her to make her so afraid of me all of a sudden!* I always kept my cool because I didn't want to show my frustration or cause a scene. They would literally have to force Isis in my car while she cried and screamed as if she was in the car with a monster and not her father. As I'm driving off, she'd continue to cry her heart out, but as soon as we get out of the parking lot, she would INSTANTLY stop crying. She would wipe away her tears and act as if nothing happened. I would give her tissue to blow her nose, and a few minutes later, she would ask things like, "What's for dinner?" and "Is Jahad coming over today?" I had never witnessed that kind of change of emotion in my life. She'd go from one extreme to the next in a matter of seconds. It freaked me out and I'd look at her, thinking to myself, *What in the hell just happened? How did she do that?* So many questions as I'd sit there, stunned. I'd carry on also as if nothing happened but I knew this type of behavior wasn't normal. This would be our routine for months, and it's sad to think that Isis put herself through that every time. This was very difficult for me to witness.

When I would pick Isis up from school, it was the total opposite. She would always have a smile on her face. She would run to get her backpack and would always give me a big hug and kiss. This was our routine. So, for the life of me, I couldn't figure out what was happening. I began dreading the days that I had to pick her up from the family business because it hurt my heart to see her act that way. I remember one day, I pulled into the parking lot at the family business to pick her up. Her mom, grandma, uncles and step grandpa were outside playing with her. She was having fun riding her bike, and I was happy to see her having fun, however, I hadn't seen her since the prior weekend, which was about four days, so I was excited to see her. When I stopped the car, one of Isis's uncles approached me and asked if they could take her to the mall for ice cream and candy. I thought, *First of all, why are you asking me this?* All of them were aware that it was my day to get Isis but instead they decided to plan something fun for her, knowing I would be there to pick her up. I didn't agree, but he continued to ask to the point where I became pissed the fuck off deep inside. I kept it to myself and politely asked Isis to get in the car. She refused, of course, because they had already put in her head that she would be going to the mall for ice cream and candy.

I couldn't believe how they set me up to look like the bad guy for not letting her go. I was furious and just seconds away from hopping out of my car to beat the shit out of her uncle for doing that sucka shit. It took a lot of strength from within to refrain from doing it. I didn't want Isis to see that side of me because then I'd really appear to be the bad guy in her eyes for whoopin' her uncle's ass. I was even ready to get down with her other uncle and grandpa because they were in on it also. I eventually lost my cool and began to cuss out the family in front of Isis. Her grandma took out her cell phone and began to record everything.

At that point, I realized it would benefit them more to see the street dude in me come out. I realized they desperately wanted a reaction from me so that they could call the police. Denise already knew I had a criminal record on file for some trouble I got into when I was eighteen years old, and any violent altercation with her family would immediately put me in jail. The odds were stacked against me, so the wisdom in me said to chill the fuck out. I calmed down and decided to call the cops. I wasn't comfortable doing it, but it was the right thing to do. The cops came, and it was a huge scene in front of the family business. I explained the story to the cops and showed them the custody agreement as proof that it was my custodial day. The cops then talked to Denise to get her side of the story, and she tried to paint a picture to imply that Isis was afraid of me and that there was no way she would let Isis be with me if Isis was afraid. Denise played the victim as if she was rescuing Isis from danger. *SMH*.

The cops explained to Denise that Isis had to go with me due to the court order, but Denise still refused. The cops wrote up a police report, and it stated that Denise refused to let Isis go with her dad on his custodial time. I was emotionally drained so I took the police report and went home. About an hour later, Denise dropped Isis off at my house. Isis walked in, crying and yelling at me, asking, "Why do you hate my mom and my grandma so much?!" I was still in shock as the chain of events started to take a toll on me emotionally. I explained to Isis that I didn't hate them and tried my best to explain what was happening.

Why are they doing this shit to me!?, is all I continued to ask myself. I've never had problems with them in the past. I was the same guy they befriended for all them years. I never changed; they did. Denise had to have told them some terrible lies about why we broke up for them to be so cold towards me. Is this type of behavior justified because I cheated? In my mind, the question was, *What came first—the chicken or the egg?* Meaning, she made me feel as though her actions against Jahad are what led me to act out in the first place. By no means am I justifying cheating, however, everyone's reaction to a situation is different, and for whatever reason that was my response. Is cheating a valid enough reason for a parent to turn their child against the other parent? I might have been a terrible boyfriend for cheating, but I was never a terrible dad to Isis. Those were the questions and thoughts that continued to linger in my head.

I started to think back to the time when Denise's mom brought out the family photos with all the pictures of Denise's real dad cut out. I started to think back to the times when Denise's dad would never talk to her mom at his sons' basketball games and all other interactions. I started to realize that Denise was treating me in a similar way her mother treated her dad after their divorce. But my case was way more extreme than his. We haven't even had our first official court date and this was where things were.

Los Angeles Police Department
INVESTIGATIVE REPORT

CHAPTER 7

The Corrupt Family Court System

A couple months had passed and now it's time for court. I waited at least three hours before we were called. Denise arrived with her mom, stepdad, and attorney. I was solo. I was prepared to present my case to the judge. I was confident without a lawyer. I had all my receipts, pictures, sign-in sheets to prove that we had a 50-50 custody agreement, health insurance proof, everything you can think of. They finally called us to the stand to swear in. The judge and Denise's lawyer began to speak in a language that I didn't understand. I was confused and waiting for my turn to speak. After ten minutes of them speaking, the judge immediately sent us to the second floor to see another mediator. We saw the mediator and could not come to an agreement so they sent us back upstairs. By that time, it was already the end of the day. We saw the judge and explained that there was no agreement made. The judge then set another court date. The date was three months out. I thought, *Why in the hell do I gotta wait three months?* I was pissed leaving the court building because now I had to go back to dealing with their shenanigans.

During the waiting period, the shenanigans started to get worse. The tension was thick on both sides, and Isis's negative behavior towards me increased. I decided to document everything that was happening so that I wouldn't forget to add it to my presentation to the judge. I received another letter in the mail for us to attend mediation before our court date. Why? Why do I have to go to another mediation when it's clear we're not able to come to an agreement on our own?

It was mediation day and I was sitting in the lobby. The elevator opened and a cop walked out. The cop stared at me, looked me up and down as if he was sizing me up. He looked at me and smirked as if he was belittling me. In my head, I thought, *What yo Blair Underwood lookin' ass lookin' at?* So I stared right back, no facial expression, as if my eyes told him, "Oh you one of them funny-style niggas." I could see in his posture that he wasn't a real one. He had that cop arrogance that immediately let me know he was a weirdo. He walked over to Denise and gave her a hug and a kiss. Clearly, this guy is her new boyfriend. I guess I was supposed to be jealous or intimated by him. *SMH.* All I could do was laugh deep inside at this corny ass nigga. A solid man wouldn't have done it that way. I wasn't surprised she'd fall for a cop. She had no clue about their history, but I did. He showed his face and left. For the third time, we could not come to any agreement at mediation.

While waiting for our court date, another incident happened during Martin Luther King weekend. Isis was with me for the weekend, but I had to work that Monday. On Sunday evening, I dropped off Isis and Jahad at one of my best friends, Jamar's house, so they can stay the night. Jamar planned to take the kids to the King parade. Isis and Jahad were excited about going because they had never been to the parade. Jahad and Isis were more like family to Jamar and his kids, and they always got excited when they could stay with the Baineses. I planned to pick them up after work and drop Isis off at her mom's later that evening.

But that Monday, I received a text from Denise at around ten in the morning, saying she was on her way to pick up Isis. I explained to her that I was at work and Isis was on her way to the King parade. I replied to Denise, letting her know that I would drop Isis off later in the evening when I got off work. She was not happy with my answer and began to question me more about Isis's whereabouts. She continued to be more demanding for answers and threatened to call the cops if I didn't tell her where Isis was. I held back from telling her because I could sense that Denise was determined to get Isis on her terms. I ultimately ignored her texts for about thirty to forty-five minutes, and she started to insanely blow up my phone, calling me back to back to back as if there was a real emergency. I thought, *What the fuck is wrong with this girl? Why is she acting like this!* I stepped away from my desk to answer the phone, and Denise was yelling and demanding I tell her where Isis was. I eventually told her she was with Jamar and that he would be taking the kids to the King parade. I explained to her again that I would bring Isis to her after I picked them up in the evening. She explained that since it was Monday, it was her custody day with Isis.

We had never discussed three-day holiday weekends in the past so I assumed Isis would stay with me for the entire weekend. More importantly, Isis was okay with it. Denise then demanded I give her Jamar's new address so that she could go get Isis. Why would she want to interrupt Isis from having a good time with her brother and cousins? Why would she be so selfish? I just didn't understand. I refused to give her Jamar's new address because I didn't wanna bring any drama to Jamar's place. I didn't want Jamar to be a part of her drama.

A couple of hours later, I got a call from Jamar saying that Denise and her mom knocked on his door and when the kids answered, Denise immediately stepped inside and took Isis out of his place. Some psycho-type shit! He was completely caught off guard because he had no idea they were coming. Jamar was just as shocked as I was. He did not chase them down or anything because it was Isis's mom. How would that look? I needed a few minutes to think and told Jamar I would call him back. I remember feeling a sense of rage that I had never felt before. My hands were shaky, my heart was pounding, and I couldn't think straight or focus. I remember going in the restroom at my job and sitting on the toilet because I didn't want anyone to see me in that state. I had no idea what was happening to me or why I was feeling that way. After about fifteen minutes, I began to calm down and gather myself.

I tried to figure out how in the hell they knew where Jamar lived. He had recently moved so there was no way for her to know where he lived. Then it came to me. It was her corny ass cop boyfriend! It had to be. He was the only person who would be able to get that kind of information based on someone's full name. All I could do was shake my head in disbelief. Denise and her mom didn't even consider Isis's feelings. They selfishly took it upon themselves to display their so-called control and power over me. It had nothing to do with Isis. It was more of a control play coming from them.

A couple of days later, I called one of my cop friends to get some insight on how they gathered information. I asked if they were able to find people's addresses by doing a name search and he confirmed. I knew it! I knew it was him. I knew he was a sucka ever since he looked at me crazy in the court building. My cop friend then asked me for her boyfriend's name. I told him his name is Luquan.

He then said out loud, "LUQUAN!?" as if he was asking and telling me that he knew him.

He then described him and I was like, "Hell yeah, that's him."

My cop friend said, "I know him. He plays on the police squad football team. His team and my team play against each other."

I was like, "For real? You know this nigga?"

He was like, "Yeah, he's hella arrogant." He explained how he didn't really like him because he'd go overboard with the shit-talking on the field. My friend then asked, "So wait, he's married to your daughter's mom?"

I was like, "No, they're not married."

He then said, "You know he's married, right?"

I was like, "MARRIED? You serious?!"

He asked me to describe Isis's mother to him, and my description was not even close. I thought, *Hell, no. This can't be for real.* He explained how after the games they would all go out for drinks and that Luquan introduced her to him as his wife. *Get the fuck outta here! This is some crazy shit.* All this time, Denise had been trying to flaunt this guy around me, and the whole time she was his side chick. A couple of days later, I decided to call one of my female friends to explain what I found out. It's always good to have female friends because they are natural detectives. I told her the story, and she immediately asked me for his name. I told her his full name and she said she would call me back. Twenty-five minutes later, she called me back and confirmed everything. She even emailed me the wedding program with photos of them together. I was like, "Damn, that's him." I eventually told all my friends and we got a good laugh about it, but it still did not change my situation with Denise. I was unsure if I should put Denise on blast or just wait. I decided to wait and kept it to myself.

We were back in court after three months, and it was finally time to see the judge. They called us up to swear in, and I was totally prepared to plead my case. Denise's attorney addressed the judge and began to say all kinds of bad things about me. She immediately painted the picture that I was an unfit person. She was shooting out lies like bullets and I was thinking, *What the fuck is she talkin' about!* Denise sat there, as quiet as a librarian, with her hands in between her legs. You'd think she was a nun from the way she was dressed. When it was her turn to speak, she spoke in a soft voice as if she was the sweetest person in the world. She continued to tell lies about my character, and I looked at her as if to say, "Who the fuck are you?" She said things like how Isis's daycare providers would tell her how sad Isis would get on the days I would pick her up, how Isis would tell them that she didn't want to leave with me, that I didn't help Isis with her homework, and that I didn't properly bathe her and wash her clothes. All lies! I couldn't take it anymore so I abruptly interjected and began to defend myself. The judge wasn't pleased, and she asked me to refrain from speaking until I was called upon. I was pissed and livid, and I couldn't refrain myself.

When it was my time to speak, I was angry and loud because I did not expect them to come out speaking in that way. I tried explaining to the judge that I simply wanted to continue the 50-50 arrangement Denise and I agreed to. I was then interjected by the judge so that she could continue to speak with the attorney. It was like they were speaking another language because I had no clue how to interpret them. I was so angry to the point where I refused to say anything else. In the end, we did not come to an agreement so the judge scheduled us to return in another three months. *Here we go again. This is some bullshit!* I was still not able to present my case. *SMH.*

During the waiting period, I continued to have issues with Isis during our exchanges. She continued to cry and act as if she didn't want to be with me when her mom was around. She continued to wait until we got outside the proximity of her mom to stop crying and act normal. It became so much of a routine that I already knew what to expect. The sad thing is Denise was never there to witness it from the inside. It's sad to know that Isis had learned to switch her behavior in order to satisfy Denise and their family. Isis felt as if she had to act out in front of them as a sign of allegiance to them. I could only imagine how hard that was for her.

ACTS OF INNAPPROPIATE BEHAVIOR BY THE PETITIONER AFTER I INFORMED HER IN MAY 2011 THAT I'LL BE REMOVING HER FROM MY HEALTH PLAN.

- I have attached a copy of an email I sent to petitioner on **Dec 27th 2011** introducing her to "Parental Alienation" with hopes that she will realize this condition and the potential effects this could have on our daughter. PAS pertains directly to our daughter and petitioner does not agree. I have highlighted all the points in the email that pertains specifically to what I'm experiencing.

- On **Oct 18th 2011** is when petitioner and I could not agree on the change of custody she proposed. I then suggested we go to the Van Nuys courthouse together the next day on **Oct 19th 2011** to seek counseling or get some assistance with our issue. Petitioner said she could not make it on the **19th** but she agreed to go the next day which was **Oct 20th 2011**. Petitioner lied to me and went to file the petition anyway on **Oct 19th 2011** and her brother served me the papers the same day. Our agreement was to go together to get help and instead she went and filed the petition first and reneged on our agreement.

- On **Jan 16th 2012** petitioner kidnapped our daughter while in my care/custody for the weekend. Our daughter was residing at my best friends home where our kids were having a play date for the Martin Luther King Holiday. My friend took the kids to the King parade and when they returned, petitioner and her mother entered his home without his approval and physically removed her from his home. Petitioner previously threatened me by saying "you're gonna make me get the authorities involved" in which the "authorities" in my opinion is her boyfriend ███████ Watkins which is a Los Angeles police officer out of the Van Nuys Department. Keep in mind that petitioner had no clue or idea of where my friend lived because he just moved from his prior residence a month before. In my opinion it's only obvious that boyfriend illegally name searched my friend and gave them his address to aid in ██████ kidnapping. My friend did not show any resistance because he did not want to cause an even bigger scene. He then notified me and I was shocked and amazed that her and her mother would do such thing when our daughter was in no danger at all. This is what prompted me to file the ex-parte motion the same week. I was denied but I felt as if it was an emergency because this whole custody battle has gone crazy. I'm just concerned about our daughters emotional state because I know she's aware that something is wrong with the relationship between her mom and dad.

- On Friday **Mar 9th 2012** I texted petitioner and asked what time can I pick our daughter up from her place since it's my weekend to be with the kids and petitioner refused to let us (my son) and I see her. Our daughter is no longer sick from the flu virus. Later I found out from our daughter on Tuesday **Mar 13th 2012** that she was with grandmother that entire weekend.

- Petitioner is also not allowing me to see our daughters report card. She presented a couple progress reports to ██████ a week ago that I have yet to see myself. It's ironic how she can pick and choose when it's ok to contact me regarding ████

- Petitioner is also refusing to allow our daughter to attend summer camp with her brother. Our daughter has expressed to me several times that she wants to attend summer camp with her brother. Her mom lied to her by saying that the school is too far away when it's not. The summer camp is called Balboa summer camp and if we mapquest both our addresses it's clear that the camp is just minutes away from where we both live.

- Petitioner will also turn off our daughters cell phone and or delete all text messages that I send to her blocking all communication with her. Ironically ██████ is now all of a sudden accusing me of these actions which is 100% a lie. Every other weekend when ████ is with her mom ████ phone will be turned off. I'll ask ████ about it and she says her mom will tell her that the battery is dead.

- On Monday **April 23rd 2012** our daughter was seen by an Allergy Specialist and her mother did not inform me of this. I had to find out from our daughter. This is very critical information pertaining to our daughters health to keep away from me.

- Petitioner is constantly passing messages to me through our daughter.

- On **Tuesday July 3rd 2012** ████ stayed the night with Jahad and I. The next day **Wednesday July 4th 2012** was a holiday and I was off from work and kids were off from school. We had planned to go to the park to barbeque and play. I figured since it's a holiday, I would at least be able to spend some time with Ivory and then bring her to her mom later around 5 or 6pm so she can spend the rest of the holiday with her other family. ████ texted me at 8:am asking me to bring Ivory to her. I respectfully asked her if I can have a little time with her since it's a holiday and she said no. ████ even called her mom and asked if she could stay with us for a little while and she still said no.

- Currently I'm scheduled to drop ████ off at her moms on Sundays at 7:pm. ████ has called her mom at least 3 consecutive Sundays asking her if she can stay the night with her brother and I. ████ would explain to her mom that I will be dropping her off to her moms place in the morning so that she can still take her to school and ████ would say no. ████ would then get upset and ask me "why don't mommy want me to stay here with you and Jahad?" I'll just tell her that one day it will change as you get older so don't worry about it for now.

- On **Wednesday October 3rd 2012** ████ sent me an email explaining to me that ████ was taken to urgent care and was tested for a UTI and was put on antibiotics for 10days. That prior weekend **Friday September 28, 2012** ████ was with me for the weekend and showing signs of having a fever and I made sure I gave her Advil fever reducer as needed. On **Sunday September 30th 2012** ███ still had a fever and was feeling sick. I explained to ███ that if she still had a fever the next **morning Monday October 1st,2012** then I would take her to the doctor. ███ was ok with that, so she called her mom that Sunday night and asked if it was ok for her to stay with me **monday** since I may have to take her to the doctor and ███ said no. That Monday morning when we awoke, ███ was still had a fever and was feeling ill. I had ███ to call her mom to explain that she was not feeling well and she asked again if she could stay with me at least until later in the morning when we can both take her to the doctor. ███ again said no and forced me to take ███ to her place anyway knowing that ███ was not feeling well and or in no position to get out of bed. Now on **Friday October 5th 2012** was again my weekend to be with the kids. ███ admitted in her email that ███ was to take her meds for 10 days but **FAILED** to send ███ medication so I can administer her medicine while she's with me. All this in attempts to paint a picture of me as bad, unfit, and uncaring parent in which is not true. Why wouldn't she send the medication?

- On **Tuesday November 6th 2012** I took ███ to get an eye exam because I noticed how she had been sitting to close to the television or reading with her books real close to her face. The eye doctor explained that her prescription has drastically changed and her glassed are outdated and need to be replaced immediately. I paid a total of $95.20 for new glasses and I've also sent a copy of the receipt to ███. ███ is also aware of the visit because she went to the doctors office the next day and they confirmed what I said was true. ███████████

- On **Friday November 9th 2012** ███ asked me to take her to her karate class the next day **Saturday November 10th, 2012.** ███ called her mom that Friday to see if we could come and pick up her karate uniform and her mom lied to her by telling her she does not have karate class on the Saturdays when she's with me. ███ told Ivory that I was more than welcomed to come on Mondays & Wednesdays at 4:pm to see her at karate class. How is that possible when I get off work at 4:30pm Mon-Fri. I also called her karate class which is named **"HOUSE OF CHAMPIONS** ███████ **"** to verify ███ schedule. They verified that ███ is on an unlimited plan and that she can attend class in her age group whenever she wants including Saturdays. ███ again lied to ███ in order to not allow me to see her attend karate.

- Kids choice Awards
- Atlanta Incident

CHAPTER 8

The Hospital Incident

On February 27, 2012, I picked up Isis from school. I noticed she was acting different, like she does when she's not feeling good. I asked her if she was feeling okay, and she said no. I checked her forehead, and I noticed she was very warm. She was no stranger to being sick often because she suffered from environmental allergies along with food allergies. There have been several times in the past when she was hospitalized due to one or the other. I was very familiar with knowing when she's sick.

We were on our way to pick up Jahad from school and then to Ralph's to pick up some quick dinner for the night. As usual, when we're at the grocery store, they always tend to put things in the basket. Sometimes I'd say no, and sometimes I'd say yes. This time, I allowed them to pick a few things so that we could hurry and get home. Then we got home, I took off my work clothes, and I started to settle in. They decide to microwave their frozen dinners so that they could eat and then start with their homework. I told Isis I would give her some Tylenol and Benadryl after she's finished eating. I was in the living room chillin', waiting for her to finish eating so that I could give her medicine for her fever. A few minutes later, she came in the living room and said she might have eaten some corn from the burrito she chose at Ralph's. Isis was highly allergic to corn and was well aware that she was not supposed to eat it. I noticed she took about two bites of the burrito. I opened the burrito and noticed that it didn't have much corn in it so I figured she'd be okay. I ended up making her a turkey sandwich, but she didn't eat that either. About fifteen minutes later, I went back in the room to give her some medicine and I noticed her eyes were really red and her body was hot. I checked her temperature and it was at 100.

I started to get worried. I gave her some Tylenol, Benadryl, and a breathing treatment with Albuterol just to be safe. This was the usual procedure for days when Isis would feel sick. It was around 7 p.m., and I told her I would check back on her in thirty minutes. When I went back to the room, I noticed that she was in the same condition. Usually, Tylenol, Benadryl, and a breathing treatment would work. I gave her another treatment, and if that didn't help, I knew I'd have to take her to the emergency room because what if she really did eat the corn from the burrito? I waited another thirty minutes and noticed she had not gotten any better. At that point, I knew it was time to take her to the ER.

Luckily, I lived literally five minutes away from Encino/ Tarzana Hospital, so we immediately got in the car and left. Once we got to the hospital, I called Denise to let her know what was going on. This was not our first rodeo with Isis being in the hospital, so I explained to Denise that if it turned out to be something serious, I'd call her. I explained to her what happened and that Isis may have eaten some corn. Denise decided to come to the hospital anyway, which is totally understandable. The nurse began to check Isis's vital signs, and her temperature had spiked to 102 so I thought maybe she did eat some corn. They drew Isis's blood to confirm if corn would be detected.

A couple of hours later, they decided to admit her. At that point, I was nervous and worried but also thankful I got her to the hospital in no time. I then contacted Qiana to let her know that Isis was being admitted and to see if I could drop off Jahad at her place. He was also no stranger to Isis being in the hospital, but it was a school night so he couldn't stay. Qiana was okay with me dropping off Jahad, so I did. Then I returned to the hospital. When I got there, they explained that Isis's temperature spiked more and that she needed to move to PICU (Pediatric Intensive Care Unit). I thought, *Damn! She must have eaten some corn.* I began to question myself. *Why didn't you read the label to be sure it was safe for her to eat? Why did you let her try something different?* Keep in mind, at the time, Isis was very aware of the foods she could not eat, and she knew how to read and check the labels. She was taught to do so. However, I still questioned myself.

While Isis was in PICU, Denise and I were still in the middle of the custody disagreement. Things were very intense between me and her family, so it was a very awkward and uncomfortable feeling for me. I put my ill feelings towards her aside and kept things cool because the focus was on Isis and not the court stuff. Denise's mother and stepdad later came to the hospital, and their energy was shitty. They were looking at me as if I was the reason that Isis was in the hospital. I tried to keep things cool, but Denise and her family immediately attempted to take control of all communication from the doctors and nurses. The doctor would ask me questions and they would immediately cut me off as if I didn't know what the hell I was talking about. They own a medical laboratory so they felt as though they were actually doctors themselves. In my head, I couldn't help but think, *What the fuck is wrong with these people? Why do they always have to do so much to be in control of everything?* It's weird because they always felt as though they could control me like they did their own adult children, but that shit would never work on me.

I found myself in another situation where I had to be the bigger person and not cause a scene in the hospital because it was about Isis and not court shit. They didn't give a fuck who or where we were, and they continued to try to cut me out. It had gotten to the point where the nurses and doctors could sense the serious tension between us. I tried my best to keep it cool and ignore them as much as possible. My focus was on Isis, and that was it. Denise and I both stayed overnight at the hospital with Isis, and we did not speak one word to each other the whole time. The next day, the nurses continued to monitor Isis as her condition was not improving. This hospital stay felt different. I could feel that this was something different in comparison to the others. I stayed with Isis the whole day as I waited for her lab test results.

The morning of the third day, I was served with more court papers. I was home freshening up and giving Denise and her family time to visit with Isis. I decided to open the letter, and it was a declaration from Denise's attorneys. In it was a statement from Denise explaining Isis's current hospitalization to the court and that I was the reason she was in the hospital. Denise explained that I was a negligent father and I allowed Isis to eat some food that she was allergic to, causing her admission in the hospital. She explained why this was the reason I did not deserve a 50-50 custody agreement as she felt I was an unfit parent. In her declaration, she also mentioned how she felt my living arrangement was not suitable for Isis, expressing that Isis shared a room with Jahad and that she was not comfortable with Isis sleeping in the same room with him because he was going through puberty. Jahad and Isis had bunk beds, so they didn't sleep in the same bed. Now this bitch done lost her damn mind. To my knowledge and experience, there is absolutely nothing abnormal about siblings sharing a room. This was very common amongst my friends with siblings and it was very common growing up. Not all families are as privileged as Denise's to afford a separate room for each kid. I'm from the black community so that was normal for us. More importantly, what the fuck was she trying to say with her statement? That since Jahad was going through puberty, she feared he would improperly touch his own sister? Disgusting! The nerve of this bitch!

She definitely crossed the line with that, and there is no way in hell I could ever respect her again. I couldn't read the rest of that bullshit in fear of what other false accusations would be in the letter. I threw the papers down on the bed and just shook my head. Isis had been in the hospital for two days, and Denise desperately took that opportunity to reach out to her attorney to draw up some papers to address to the court. Man! Unbelievable! I made my way back to the hospital and when I arrived at the room, Denise and her mom were crying because Isis's condition had gotten worse. Isis developed pneumonia, her face began to swell, and she could not breathe on her own.

The doctors said in order for Isis to live, they'd have put her on a ventilator machine to pump extra air into her lungs. I began to panic because I had no idea what that meant. All I knew was that it was bad. Very bad. My heart rate increased, my hands were sweaty, and I couldn't think straight. I couldn't focus on anything. All I could think of was Isis better not die. The doctor told us we had to leave the room and nobody could be present when they inserted the ventilator. I went to the waiting room to try to relax and calm down, but I just couldn't. I felt horrible. She was only six years old, and it crushed me to know that I couldn't save her. My heart continued to race as I slipped in and out of consciousness. I felt like I was having a heart attack. I could barely breathe because of my thoughts that she won't make it. I had nobody there with me for support, so I had to fight through my emotions on my own.

About thirty minutes later, the doctor came out and explained that the ventilator had been inserted and that Isis was now stable. He said she was unconscious and that she would not be able to respond to us. I was struggling with my emotions while trying to stay strong. When I walked in the room, I felt like I was in a horror movie. I remember seeing Isis lying flat on this metal-like bed, with her head looking upwards into a bunch of bright lights beaming on her small frame. As I got closer, I saw this big tube stuck down her throat, and her eyes were taped shut. I could still see her swollen eyes under the tape. There was some gel-like stuff in her eyes to prevent them from drying out. Her whole body was swollen as if she had gained weight in a matter of minutes. To me, it looked like she was dead. I was in so much shock that I immediately walked out of the room. I was afraid to touch her. She didn't look the same. I wished I could trade places with her. I had never seen anything like that in my life, and since it was my child, I was devastated.

I remember sitting on a chair next to the waiting room, crying my heart out. The door was still open, and from a short distance I could still see Isis lying there, stiff as if she were dead. A couple of nurses came to console me, telling me that everything would be alright. I could not stop shaking; it was too intense for me. Minutes later, I heard some voices walking through the door. I remember a hand being extended to me, and when I looked up, it was Luquan, Denise's boyfriend. He reached out to shake my hand, but I wasn't in the mindset to shake his hand. I left his hand hanging there, and he then said to me, "What? You don't shake hands?" I looked at him in disbelief, thinking, *How could you be so disrespectful at a time like this?* I said, "Get the fuck out of my face." He then walked to the room with Denise and put his arms around her in a disrespectful manner. They made it a point to stop right at the door to kiss and hug, right in the middle of Isis and me. I already knew he was a sucka, but for me to see Denise engage in that type of behavior in that setting was sadly disappointing. I felt like she was trying to make me jealous or something. If so, she was just wasting her time.

They eventually moved Isis from that room to a regular room, and from there I was able to slowly relax. I held Isis's hand, gave her kisses, and talked to her. They said she was unconscious, but in my mind, she could hear me loud and clear. After about twenty-five or thirty minutes, I decided to step out to get some fresh air. As I walked past the waiting room, I noticed officer Luquan sitting down, texting from his phone. I walked in the room and said to him, "How could you be so disrespectful at time like this? You a foul ass nigga." Then I walked out.

I went outside to walk around. I couldn't get the image of Isis lying on the bed in that room out of my head. It just wouldn't leave. I later made my way back up to Isis. A couple of hours later, the nurse came in with Isis's lab results. He explained to us that Isis tested negative for digestion of corn or any food allergy. He said there was no trace of it in her bloodstream. He proceeded to explain to us that Isis tested positive for H1N1, which is a deadly virus known as the swine flu. I've never heard of H1N1 so I had no idea what he meant. All I knew was it was serious. Denise and her mom were visibly shaken by the news, and I could feel how serious it was. I asked the nurse if she would be okay and he said yes, but it will take some time. I let out a huge sigh of relief knowing that Isis would be okay. It was hard to see her in that condition, but she's a strong girl so I knew she would pull through.

Later that night, when the nurse returned to check on Isis, he asked if he could pray over Isis with me. I thought it was a beautiful gesture and of course I said yes. It was just the nurse, Isis, and me in the room at the time, and I felt a lot better after his prayer. Since the room was empty, the nurse thanked me for bringing Isis to the ER when I did. He said if it would've been a day or two later, she wouldn't have survived. He continued to explain how he sensed the tension between Denise's family and me, and he commended me for the way I was handling the situation. He told me I was Isis's hero because I had saved her life. In that moment, I could feel a ton of anxiety being released from my body. All along I felt I was the reason she ended up in the hospital. I started to think back to that day when I picked her up from school. I remembered that she was already acting sick and she already had a fever before she even ate anything. It all made sense and I felt even better about my decision to take her to the ER.

The next day, family and friends were allowed to visit. Out of respect when Denise's family and friends came to see Isis, I stepped out so that they could spend time with her. However, when my friends came by to see Isis, Denise's family showed no respect. They stayed in the room the whole time as if they were protecting Isis from danger, as if my friends meant nothing to Isis. It was some weirdo shit for real. I couldn't understand how they could be so selfish under those conditions. I explained to my friends ahead of time that Denise's folks would be acting like they controlled the situation, but I knew my people would pay them no mind anyway. They were totally disrespectful and I will never forget that.

Later in the evening, Qiana and Jahad came to see Isis. Jahad was visibly sad to see her in that condition. After a few minutes, he gained some courage and finally held Isis's hand to speak to her. While Jahad was speaking to Isis, her hand began to move as if she was trying to respond to him. Miraculously she felt her brother's presence. The whole time while Isis was on the ventilator, she didn't move for anyone. It felt like a scene from a movie. It seemed as if she could really hear his voice. It was a special moment for sure. Jahad had a follow-up doctor appointment after his visit with Isis. Fortunately, his appointment was in the same facility where Isis was being treated.

While we waited to be called, I started telling Qiana how the doctor explained to me that Isis was not sick from food allergy digestion but from H1N1. I also vented my frustration about how selfish and disrespectful Denise's family was. I also told Qiana about my run-in with Denise's cop boyfriend and how disrespectful he was too. As I was telling the story, Qiana asked if I knew Denise's boyfriend's name. I said, "Yeah, his name is Luquan." She looked at me as if she knew him already.

She then asked if he worked at the Van Nuys police station and if he lived in Palmdale. I wondered why she was asking me all this. I said, "Yeah, he work at the Van Nuys station and I think he do live in Palmdale." Qiana said, "OMG, Erin is dating him." Erin is Qiana's best friend who introduced me to Qiana back in the day. I said, "What!? Are you sure?" Qiana started to describe him and from her description it was definitely him. His name is not common and when she heard it, she had a feeling it was him. I said, "Call Erin right now!"

She called Erin and then gave me the phone to speak to her. Erin confirmed it was him and she mentioned how he had texted her last night to see if he could see her. We were all in disbelief. Erin sent me a screenshot of his texts to her, and the texts were sent at the exact same time I approached him in the waiting area where I noticed he was on his phone texting. Unbelievable! He knew Denise would be staying the night at the hospital. I can't make this shit up. After Jahad's appointment, I went back to Isis's room to check on her. The doctor finally hit us with some good news. He mentioned how Isis's condition was positively improving and the next morning they would remove the ventilator. A huge sigh of relief. The following day, the ventilator was removed and a couple days later, on March 6, 2012, Isis was released from the hospital.

PROVIDENCE TARZANA MEDICAL CENTER
18321 Clark Street
Tarzana, CA 91356

Patient Name: JONES███
Med Rec #:███

Age: 6
Room: FPICU1

DOB:

Admission Date: 02/27/12
Discharge Date: 03/06/12

FINAL DIAGNOSES:
1. H1N1 infection.
2. Respiratory failure.
3. Status asthmaticus.
4. Hypoxemia resolved.
5. Methicillin-resistant Staphylococcus aureus colonization.
6. Multiple allergies.
7. Very elevated Immunoglobulin E.

SECONDARY DIAGNOSES:
1. Methicillin-resistant Staphylococcus aureus colonization respiratory failure resolved.
2. Multiple allergies.

COMPLICATIONS:
None. She did require mechanical ventilation from the H1N1 infection and status asthmaticus.

RIEF HISTORY:
The patient is a beautiful 6-year-old female who was admitted on February 27 with wheezing. Initially, it was thought that it was secondary to ingestion of allergen. However, later it became evident that she had status asthmaticus from H1N1 infection with fever and respiratory failure.

HOSPITAL COURSE:
She continued to deteriorate. After admission, she was intubated. She had a femoral line placed. She required had high settings of terbutaline drip, Tamiflu, Solu-Medrol, Pulmicort, Versed drip, fentanyl drip, and continuous albuterol.

Patient's lung condition slowly improved. She was given a restricted diet because of her multiple allergies.

The patient had multiple therapies, breathing treatments, education. Her IgA level was found to be very high.

She was eventually extubated on or about March 2, and continued to improve.

On March 3, her terbutaline drip was decreased, her albuterol drip was decreased, Solu Medrol was decreased. Oxygen was decreased, and her Foley was out, and her central venous catheter was out.

She continued to improve, and she was eventually weaned to room air, and her steroids were decreased.

JONES███

Tarzana Discharge Summary
Page 1 of 2

CHAPTER 9

The Child Support Scam

Denise and I had another court date just two days after Isis was discharged. As we waited in the courtroom lobby, Denise's attorney came to me to discuss an arrangement. She explained how it was not a good time for me and Denise to continue to fight since we were both still emotionally overwhelmed from Isis's hospital stay. She suggested that I agree to a "temporary custody order" and that she would ask the judge to reschedule our hearing based on the circumstance. She suggested that I agree to one overnight visit and every other weekend. She suggested it would go in effect in a few weeks to give Isis time to heal. During that time, my focus was on Isis and I couldn't care less about court stuff. I just wanted to see Isis get better. I made it clear that if I signed a "temporary custody order" based on our circumstance, it was only "temporary" until our next hearing. She said yes. She made it very clear that it was only temporary in order for us to focus on Isis's wellbeing. In my mind, I felt like she was being sincere and it was the right thing to do, so I signed the "temporary" agreement.

We then went in to see the judge. Her attorney explained to the judge that we were able to come to an agreement, but she failed to mention "temporary." She failed to mention what we agreed on in the waiting area. I then interrupted and tried to explain to the judge that we made an agreement to reschedule the hearing because of the situation. The judge then told me that since I signed the agreement, the order would be permanent. I said, "Permanent!?" I yelled at Denise's attorney to let her know that she was wrong for what she did. She lied to me. She made me believe it was a temporary order. On the paper, it even said "temporary order." The judge then gave me some fake ass apology and suggested I hire an attorney if I wanted to continue to fight for more custodial time with Isis.

I couldn't believe what just happened. Our daughter almost died a couple days prior and then they go and pull this shit. They had no sympathy at all for what just happened to Isis. Denise's attorney took my vulnerability and used it as a loophole to benefit her client. I began to realize that family court was not in the best interest of Isis. I started to become aware of how the family court system is set up to benefit and profit from custody disputes. They continuously set court dates three to four months out for their job security.

What they fail to realize is during these long wait periods, children, parents, and families suffer emotionally and financially from their tactics. I started having health issues due to the stress from the chain of events. I would stay up until like two to three in the morning every day, trying to make sense of it all. I couldn't understand where the extreme intense hate came from by Denise and her family. Why are they exhausting every bit of their money and energy for me not to have equal time with Isis? Why are they sending so many negative frequencies into her mind to turn her against me? Why? Why are they brainwashing her? Why are they not considering her feelings when they know how much Isis enjoys spending time with me? Why do they want to take that away from her? How could they be so selfish?

I started experiencing heart palpitations and nightmares, and I would wake up in cold sweats almost every morning. I was diagnosed with high blood pressure and generalized anxiety disorder (GAD). I was prescribed Xanax and other types of meds which I stopped taking because they made me feel weird. I didn't like the side effects. I would become very moody and distant, and I didn't like not being in control of my thoughts. I felt uncomfortably different so I stopped with the meds. I had no idea the court process would be so emotionally draining. All I wanted was equal time with Isis. That's it and that's all.

I had no choice but to hire an attorney. I knew it would be expensive and I definitely couldn't afford one. I had to withdraw $3,000 from my 401k to put down as a retainer. The attorney's rate was $175 an hour. Wow! I couldn't afford that shit, but I had no choice. Fortunately, for Denise, her mom and stepdad paid all her attorney fees. *SMH*. A few weeks later, I received a letter from the California State Department of Child Support Services. Now I had to deal with child support. Since I was lied to and tricked into signing the temporary custody order, Denise would have seventy percent custody time and I would have thirty percent. Since Denise would have more time with Isis, I would have to pay her child support.

The child support guidelines are based on a system called DissoMaster. It somehow calculates time spent, income, and child care expenses, and then it would automatically spit out a number. My child support was set to $800 a month. I was thinking, *How in the hell am I gonna afford $800 a month, attorney fees, and the basic cost of my living expenses?* I tried explaining to the child support officer that there was no way I could afford to pay that. I explained to them that I also have 50-50 custody of Jahad and that $800 a month would immediately impact my financial obligations to him. I explained how $800 a month would basically put me on the streets. I asked for some leniency because it wasn't fair that Jahad and Qiana would now be affected by this and they have nothing to do with it. They did not consider the fact that I also paid rent, which provided a roof over their heads. I also brought food and lunch for Isis to take to school, clothes, daycare, health insurance, etc. I shared the same expenses as Denise did, and it was not even close to $800 a month. Jahad's expenses were not even close to $800 a month so I knew it was some bullshit. It felt like I was being extorted by child support. I felt like I was being punished for being financially able to support Isis.

Denise's argument was that the only reason I wanted equal time with Isis is so that I wouldn't have to pay child support. No! How about because I love her and any loving parent would want to spend as much time with their child as possible. They pretty much looked at me like, "Oh well, that's your problem. You figure it out." They gave zero fucks about that. To me it was their way of saying, "Fuck you and your son." There was no way I could voluntarily pay $800 a month. Doing so would immediately put me out on the streets. How in the hell do they expect me to provide for my children if I wouldn't be able to take care of myself?

A few months later, child support began garnishing my pay checks. It immediately put me in tons of debt. I maxed out all of my credit cards and cashed out my 401k only to temporarily stay afloat. I struggled to provide food for us. My eighty-year-old grandma sent me her food card so I could use it until I could get back on my feet. There were times when Qiana would send food for us to eat as well. I appreciate everyone so much for all their support. They have no idea how much it helped and got us through. I had gotten months behind on rent and ultimately, I was served with eviction papers along with a letter to vacate from the Los Angeles Sheriff Department. I eventually had to borrow money from family and friends to attend civil court to avoid eviction.

What's worse is that child support even put a hold on Jahad's checking account because my social security number was linked to his high school checking account. Jahad had about $3,000 in his account, which he won from a game show he was on. He was buying some food after school one day and his card was declined. He called me upset and confused. I didn't even know what happened until I called the bank and they explained it was a child support hold. I was super pissed! Livid! How could they take money from him when he's not involved in the case? They eventually released the hold, but it's scary to know that child support has so much power and control over your finances. Child support is one big money extortion scandal. Even if you're a good father or parent, they are relentless in their pursuit to suck every dollar out of you. All I could do was shake my head in disbelief and keep it moving.

NOTICE TO VACATE

CASE NUMBER: _13B00750_

TO: Judgment debtor, members of the judgment debtor's household, and any occupants residing with the judgment debtor.

By virtue of a *Writ of Possession of Real Property*, a copy of which is attached,

YOU ARE ORDERED TO VACATE THE PREMISES DESCRIBED IN THE WRIT NOT LATER THAN: _3/18/13_, 20 ____.

SHERIFF'S BRANCH (Name, Address and Telephone Number)

☐ SHERIFF'S DEPARTMENT
14400 ERWIN ST. MALL
VAN NUYS, CA 91401

☐ LEROY D. BACA, SHERIFF

By: ___________________

Date: _3/13/13_ Deputy

☐ ☐

76N654E SH-CI-52 (REV. 9/94)

NOTICE TO VACATE

4. **Judgment debtor** *(name, type of legal entity stated in judgment if not a natural person, and last known address):*

KENYADA JONES
17910 Burbank Blvd., #220
Encino, CA 91316

☐ Additional judgment debtors on next page

5. **Judgment entered on** *(date):* MAR 0 1 2013

6. ☐ **Judgment renewed on** *(dates):*

7. **Notice of sale** under this writ
  a. ☒ has not been requested.
  b. ☐ has been requested *(see next page).*
8. ☐ Joint debtor information on next page.

[SEAL]

9. ☒ See next page for information on real or personal property to be delivered under a writ of possession or sold under a writ of sale.
10. ☐ This writ is issued on a sister-state judgment.
11. Total judgment .... $ POSSESSION ONLY
12. Costs after judgment (per filed order or memo CCP 685.090) .... $ __________
13. Subtotal *(add 11 and 12)*............ $ __________
14. Credits .... $ __________
15. Subtotal *(subtract 14 from 13)* .... $ __________
16. Interest after judgment (per filed affidavit CCP 685.050) (not on GC 6103.5 fees). . . $ __________
17. Fee for issuance of writ .... $ __________
18. **Total** *(add 15, 16, and 17)*........... $ __________
19. Levying officer:
  (a) Add daily interest from date of writ *(at the legal rate on 15)* (not on GC 6103.5 fees) of .... $ __________
  (b) Pay directly to court costs included in 11 and 17 (GC 6103.5, 68637; CCP 699.520(i)) .... $ __________
20. ☐ The amounts called for in items 11–19 are different for each debtor. These amounts are stated for each debtor on Attachment 20.

Issued on *(date):* MAR 0 1 2013 Clerk, by ___________________ , Deputy

NOTICE TO PERSON SERVED: SEE NEXT PAGE FOR IMPORTANT INFORMATION.

Page 1 of 2

Form Approved for Optional Use
Judicial Council of California
EJ-130 [Rev. January 1, 2012]

WRIT OF EXECUTION

Code of Civil Procedure, §§ 699.520, 712.010, 715.010
Government Code, § 6103.5

CHAPTER 10

Parental Alienation

At this point, Isis had fully recovered from her hospital stay. I planned for Jahad and Isis to visit my mom in Atlanta for the upcoming summer. Initially, Denise didn't agree with the dates I selected because her mom had just moved to a new house and they planned a housewarming the weekend Isis would be in Atlanta. I had already confirmed with Denise a month prior and had already purchased their plane tickets. Denise was upset about it and eventually agreed to let Isis go because I purchased their tickets before they scheduled the housewarming.

Jahad and Isis had been to Atlanta a couple times before, and they would always be excited to go. My mom would have fun activities planned for the week. When they arrived in Atlanta, my mom called me to tell me that Isis was acting distant towards her. She said Isis didn't really speak to her and that Isis was reluctant to give her a hug. I told my mom to give her a little time and she'll eventually open up. The next day, Isis called me and she was super excited and happy because my mom took them swimming at the neighbor's house. Isis loves swimming. She was extra happy because they had a diving board, and she told me she did a front flip off of the diving board for the first time. It was refreshing to hear how happy she was being that the hospital incident was just months before.

Unfortunately, my excitement was short lived because Isis called me later that night, crying and saying that she was ready to come back to LA. I asked her why and she said someone by the pool was upset with her because she splashed water on them. I started thinking to myself, *Hmmm. Who would be upset about that, especially if they were all at the pool?* Her answer didn't sound right but she continued to ask to come back to LA. I then asked her to put Jahad on the phone so I could ask him what happened. Jahad told me that after they ate dinner, Denise and her mom called Isis. He said she went downstairs to talk to them for a while, and when she went back upstairs, her entire mood changed. He said she was acting just fine before she spoke to them. I then called my mom to try and get more information, and she said the exact same thing. Jahad and my mom denied that someone was upset with Isis for splashing water on them. She made up that story and I was confused as to why she would say that.

Then I figured it out. Denise or her mom must have made Isis feel guilty about her not being at their housewarming. I don't know exactly what was said, but it was clearly upsetting her enough to sway her mood. I was livid and pissed because I knew it was them that said something to her to make her feel that way. They are sick! Why the fuck would they do something like that to her? The next morning, I spoke to Isis and her mood was still the same. I explained to her that the people from the pool didn't mean to hurt her feelings (although it wasn't true) and that she didn't have to go there ever again. We made an agreement that she would give it one more day and if she still wanted to leave then we would let her come back. I was hoping and praying that she would change her mind because my mom had planned to take them on a tour to the Coca-Cola factory. I called Jahad later in the day to check to see how she was, and he explained that she was still the same. He said she didn't want to participate in any of the activities. I could tell that Jahad was upset with Isis because she was taking away from his fun.

Ultimately, their trip was cut short because Isis continued to act as if she didn't wanna be there. Later that evening, I got a call from Denise telling me that she would fly out to Atlanta to get Isis. Her tone was as if Isis was in some kind of danger and it was urgent that she see Isis. My brain couldn't process what was happening. I was pissed and in disbelief that they would sabotage Isis's trip like that. My mom was totally confused and sad because she didn't know what to do or how to make Isis feel better. Jahad was also upset, sad, and confused.

The very next day, Denise flew to Atlanta to "rescue" Isis. *SMH.* Isis was there only two days. I began to reflect on the previous chain of events caused by Denise and her family, which led me to do some research. I started Googling things pertaining to the situation, and that's where I was introduced to Parental Alienation Syndrome (PAS). I was immediately blown away by what I was reading. In short, parental alienation is a set of strategies that a parent uses to foster a child's rejection of the other parent. Parental Alienation Syndrome develops in children who come to hate, fear, and reject the targeted parent as someone unworthy of having a relationship with them (Social Work Today, 2008). Boom! This is it! I continued to read more and more, and every single description of PAS had already happened and continued to happen to me. I read and watched videos nonstop for a week straight and I was convinced this is what was happening to me and Isis.

I learned about narcissism and narcissistic behavior. It all made sense. I remember sending Denise an email explaining to her that I felt she was alienating Isis from me. I attached articles on PAS, hoping she would identify with the description and that it would resonate with her because ultimately it was Isis who was being emotionally abused and affected by it. This was my last hope. Denise responded to my email, saying, "Please don't email things that don't pertain to Isis." I thought, *What the fuck?!* This has everything to do with Isis. I then reached out to my attorney and explained to her that parental alienation is what I wanted to address in court. The next court date was months away, and between that time and the court date, there were several more incidents that occurred.

On January 9, 2012, I received a confirmation email from the director of the Star Program at Isis's school. The Star Program was a performing arts afterschool program where you would need to be selected to attend. Not every kid was accepted. Isis always mentioned how she wanted to be in the program. I talked to the front office staff at her school to find out how to enroll and I did. I emailed Denise the confirmation email, and not to my surprise, she made up an excuse for why Isis couldn't attend. I was paying $260 per month for Creative Kids, which was her afterschool program at the time and she only attended one to two days per week. The Star Program was free of charge. Denise said it would interfere with Isis's swimming and piano classes. BULLSHIT! Isis had already mentioned to me that she preferred to attend the Star Program over piano classes.

The Star Program was a big thing for kids, and Isis really wanted to be a part of it. Fortunately, I never told her that I signed her up and that she was accepted because I had a feeling Denise would have an excuse for why she couldn't attend. Isis's feelings would have been hurt, and it's sad just to think about it. Months later, I got a call from my homie, John, inviting Isis to go to the Nickelodeon Awards with his daughter at the Forum in Inglewood. John's daughter's name is Tuesday. Isis and Tuesday have been good friends since they were born. John explained to me that he had VIP tickets for them. The VIP tickets were exclusive and it would give them access to all the activities for the evening. Isis loved Nickelodeon so I knew she would be more than excited to go, especially with Tuesday.

When I broke the news to her, she was ecstatic! Her face was filled with excitement and she couldn't wait to go.

The event was on a Wednesday from 4 p.m. to 8:30 p.m. Wednesday was Denise's day to have Isis. I sent Denise an email asking if Isis could attend. John also offered to pick up Isis from school to take her and I would meet them there after work. I explained to Denise that I would drop Isis off at her place immediately after the event. I felt there was no way she would make up an excuse for this one. Everyone knew how much Isis loved Nickelodeon and that it was her favorite channel. Well, I was wrong. Denise responded, saying Isis shouldn't be out so late on a school night. She also said she didn't feel comfortable with John taking her and that I would not be there. So I asked her to take Isis instead. She said she would not be able to leave work early. More BULLSHIT!

I explained to her that the event happens only once a year and Isis was really looking forward to going. I understood it was a school night, but this should have been an exception to the rule because it's a fun event to celebrate kids. It's amazing how thousands of parents let their kids attend. I'm sure Denise was the only parent out of thousands who would not let their kid attend because it was a school night. *SMH.* When I broke the news to Isis, she was crushed. I had a talk with her and asked her to talk to her mom about it. I told Isis to let her mom know how much she really wanted to go and maybe she would change her mind. The following morning, I dropped off Isis at her mom's place, and as Isis walked in, she looked backed to me and crossed her fingers in hopes she would be able to go.

Later that night, I texted Isis to get the results and, unfortunately, Denise would not agree to let her go. At that point, I decided to never ask Denise to let Isis attend any event during her custodial time, even if it was weeks in advance. However, I always made it clear that I would have no issues with Isis attending any event with Denise during my custody time if we had no prior plans. There were so many events Isis missed out on over the years. *SMH*. Very sad.

It was time for yet another court appearance. This would be the eighth or ninth appearance in a few years now. At this point, I was roughly at $20,000 in debt in lawyer fees, which is extremely low compared to Denise's $100,000 balance, and growing. It is insane to know that her family is willing to pay this kind of money to avoid me spending extra time with Isis. INSANE! We got to court, and as usual, we got sworn in as the attorneys prepared to battle. My attorney addressed parental alienation to the judge. She addressed how Denise's behavior related to parental alienation. She gave countless examples of parental alienation and how it directly applied to me.

Of course, Denise's attorney interjected and disagreed with my attorney. The judge didn't seem too convinced that parental alienation was taking place. However, she did seem to be interested and allowed my attorney to finish her explanation. Denise's attorney presented a video of Isis not wanting to get in the car with me during a routine pick-up. Denise had the nerve to record the exchange so that the judge could see for herself that Isis did not want to go with me. It's funny how Denise was one hundred percent okay with the custody schedule where I receive less time, but when it comes to equal time she would go far and beyond to create so many roadblocks and false narratives painting me to be some bad guy. It was very hard to wrap my brain around what possessed Denise. She acted as if she was completely controlled by an evil spirit. I couldn't even look at her anymore because she was a totally different person. Her appearance was the same but her spirit was in a dark place.

The judge decided that it would be best for Isis to testify in court. I didn't think it was necessary for a ten-year-old to testify against her own father. It made no sense to me. I felt that she was not emotionally and mentally mature enough to totally understand what was going on. Ultimately, I had no say, so I agreed to let Isis testify against me. In my mind, I could already see how her testimony would play out. I was livid! Not because of what she would say but more so because of the fact that the judge would even allow a minor to testify after I just expressed my concern of parental alienation. Again, the court date was set for another three to four months out, allowing more time for the alienation process to get stronger.

So there I was again four months later. We entered the courtroom, and this time, the judge cleared out all the people in the room and made it a private matter. Isis was there, sitting on her grandmother's lap. Denise's stepdad was also in attendance. The judge called Isis to the front of the room and began to ask her questions. She started with simple questions to try to make Isis feel comfortable. Isis was very shy and soft-spoken. She didn't want to answer any questions so she answered with one or two words. It was difficult to get Isis to speak at first, but eventually she started to talk more. The judge asked questions like, "What do you do for fun when you're with your dad? Does your dad help you with homework? Do you enjoy being with your dad?" Things of that nature so that the judge can get an idea about my parenting. Isis never said one bad thing about me. She also asked Isis the same questions about Denise.

At the end of the testimony, the judge asked Isis if she would be okay with spending more time with me, and she said no. Isis said she wanted to keep the schedule as it is. How would she even know to say that? If she was okay with the current schedule, why wouldn't she be okay with an additional night? These were questions that I could never get a valid answer to from the judge. In my mind, it was clear as day what was happening to me. For the life of me, I could not understand why the court continued to drag this on and not acknowledge my concerns. In the end, the judge ordered a full 730 custody evaluation. The custody evaluator would determine if an additional overnight visit with me was reasonable.

PEOPLE WHO HAVE NOT BEEN TO FAMILY COURT THINK...

Lawyers and judges do what is best for the children. They rely on evidence and the truth. They would never put a child in a dangerous situation. They follow the laws.

PEOPLE WHO HAVE BEEN TO FAMILY COURT KNOW...

Lawyers and judges are totally corrupt. They do not follow the laws. They have no rules, no trial. They put kids with abusive parents. They do not look at evidence. They do not care about the children. It's an insane, crazy house circus without rules. They act like insane lunatics and treat everyone like criminals. They destroy the lives of children and parents.

– Unknown

CHAPTER 11

The Fraudulent Custody Evaluator

A 730 custody evaluation is conducted by a psychologist who evaluates both parents as well as the children involved, family members, and friends. It also involves psychological tests, home visits, and health and school records. Custody evaluators make specific visitation recommendations to the court based on their final analysis. I've never heard of a custody evaluation until then, and when my attorney explained it, I figured it would be a good idea. Custody evaluators are supposed to be "neutral and non-biased" to either side. I began to feel better because I felt that a psychologist with experience in custody disputes would be the perfect person for our situation.

I couldn't wait to get started until I learned that custody evaluations are very expensive and I was required to pay half the cost. The judge explained we could either find a private custody evaluator or a court-appointed evaluator. Custody evaluations range from $1,000 to $20,000. The cost for our custody evaluation was a whopping $10,000. Since I could not afford to pay half, the judge ordered Denise's parents to pay it as they were already fully funding her attorney fees. At the time, I didn't think anything of it, but I later I found out our custody evaluator worked with Denise's attorney in the past. They had a client referral relationship, which basically means the evaluator will give favorable results to the attorney no matter the outcome.

We were required to take the Minnesota Multiphasic Personality Inventory-2 (MMPI-2) psychology test. It's used as an additional source of hypothesis about the individual being evaluated. Denise's results had an elevation of the L (lie) and of the K (defensiveness) validity scales. Her pattern of responses suggested that she tends to present herself in a consistently favorable light and as being relatively free of common shortcomings to which most people will admit. Prior to the test, I consistently explained to the judge how her crazy accusations aren't true. Her results proved me right, however, this part of the test was somehow scored as "invalid" by the custody evaluator. Go figure.

Family court is a tricky business filled with hidden agendas designed to suck every dollar out of you, all in the name of the "best interest of the child." It's a dirty and crooked system. Our custody evaluation lasted three months. It started on October 9, 2013 and ended on January 7, 2013. In the end, it was very clear that the custody evaluator was biased and favored Denise. The custody evaluator stated in the report that after further review, she did not see a good enough reason to allow Isis an additional overnight visit with me and Jahad. It was also stated that there were no signs of parental alienation. Really? Not even one sign? Unbelievable. I one hundred percent disagreed with the final findings. However, for me to rebut the evaluator's decision would ultimately cost more money. I would have to hire another mental health professional to interview/cross-examine the evaluator in court. Since they were well aware of my financial status, they knew I was not in a position to challenge. This is another tactic the family court would use to keep the feud alive and put more money into their pocket.

A few months later after the custody evaluation, we attended court. This time it was to go over the evaluator's findings. To my surprise, the judge expressed how she felt in some ways Denise was being manipulative and controlling of Isis. Finally, I felt some sort of relief. This time I was able to be quiet and listen as the judge scolded Denise about her behavior. In the end, the judge was in my favor. She issued a "step up" plan, which over time would allow me to slowly increase my time with Isis again. The judge suggested that I send Denise an email asking her if I could take Isis out to lunch after her softball games during her custodial time. Just lunch for about an hour and I would drop Isis off at Denise's. Denise did not agree and argued that Isis wouldn't want me to take her to lunch after her game. The judge scolded her more and explained to her that she needed to figure out a way to let Isis know it was okay for her to go to lunch with me. Sounds crazy, right?

The following week after court, I sent Denise an email asking her if I could take Isis out to lunch after her upcoming softball game. Denise replied and said that she already made plans with Isis after her game. I replied back, saying, "Ok, maybe next time." For four months straight, I emailed Denise asking if I could take Isis to lunch after her game and every single time she replied with an excuse. I never got to take Isis to lunch. So there we were, back in court again for an update on how things have been going with the step up plan. I printed out all the emails I sent to Denise and my attorney gave them to the judge to read. The judge was upset and disappointed that I was not able to take Isis to lunch at least once in four months. She scolded Denise some more and ultimately increased my custodial time to forty percent. I wanted fifty percent, but after seven years of going back and forth to court, getting counseling and evaluations, etc., etc., I didn't wanna fight anymore. I was ready to accept it and put the nightmare behind me.

Denise and her family were not happy with the decision. She broke down and cried as if the judge just released Isis to a murderer. She was visibly angry at the judge and I had a gut feeling this thing was still not over. The step up plan was set to go in effect at the end of the school year, which was going to be in about three months. I was finally able to walk out of the courtroom with a sense of relief after seven years of custody battle.

CHAPTER 12

Trauma

Within the three months, I noticed Isis's behavior worsened. When I picked her up from school, she wouldn't even say hi or talk to me. When we got home, she'd go straight to her room, close the door, and only came out to eat and use the bathroom. She did this every weekend during my custodial time. It saddened me to the point where I would cry every night because I didn't know what to do. I repeatedly questioned God because I couldn't comprehend his reasoning for allowing this to happen. I became very angry at God. My faith in God slowly diminished. I've been fighting this battle for seven years and he didn't intervene. I had nobody to talk to. My anxiety heightened to the point where I would have nightmares of Isis killing me in my sleep. I'd wake up in cold sweats. I became paranoid. Family and friends would empathize, but no one can ever feel this type of pain or understand parental alienation unless it happened to them. She completely removed herself from me physically and emotionally.

The week when my increased custody time was to begin is when things escalated to the unimaginable. It was a Sunday night at around 8:30 p.m. I received a text from Denise saying that she's on her way to pick up Isis. Keep in mind it was my custodial weekend. She said Isis called her and asked if she could pick her up because she was afraid I would harm her. She said Isis was crying and that I made her stay in her room with no food for the whole day. I explained to Denise that none of what she said is true. Just two weeks prior, I had taken Isis and her friend to Six Flags and we had a blast. At Six Flags, Isis had totally forgotten how she's been treating me. She was my daughter again. We laughed, rode roller coasters, played games, everything! So for her to say those things baffled me.

I explained to Denise that I would drop Isis off the following morning as I normally did. It's ironic how all of a sudden this happened the week I was to begin my increased time. Minutes later, Denise texted me to let me know that she was outside. I went to Isis's room and explained to her that I would drop her off in the morning. She began to cry and asked why I wouldn't let her go with her mom. Denise kept calling my phone and I ignored her phone calls. She then called Isis's phone and told her to just walk out. Isis tried to walk out, but I did not let her leave. She started to cry more and told me that she hated me and that she never wanted to see me again. Denise then came to my door and started banging on it, yelling, "Let Isis out! Let her out!" as if she was really in danger.

All of a sudden, an emotional rage flared up inside me. Panic, anxiety, and anger took control of me. "Fuck yo mama!" I screamed out loud. "Fuck her! Why can't you see that she's trying to take you away from me?" I said to Isis. I grabbed her by her arm and took her back to her room. Tears were uncontrollably falling from her eyes as I tried to give her a hug and apologize for what I said. She resisted and tried to fight me. She was visibly shaken up as she's never seen me in that way before. We both cried as I tried to console her. I repeatedly told her I love her and that I was sorry for scaring her. It was an out-of-body experience for me. Something took over me. I didn't physically harm her, but I could tell my words hurt her as if I did.

When I looked into Isis's eyes as she continued to fight her way out of the room, I saw Denise in her. It's hard to put into words but I saw all of Denise's evil energy transfer into Isis's soul. She was not Isis anymore. She became Denise. I looked at her in shock and disbelief. She turned into someone else, just like Denise did when this custody battle began. At that point, I knew it was over and that I'd never see Isis again for a long time. I forced myself to hug Isis against her will and told her how much I loved her and that none of it was her fault. I held her so tight because I knew this was the end. I heard additional knocking on my door and it was the police. "Open the door!" the officer yelled. I was in some kind of trance because everything was happening in super slow motion. I ignored the officer and continued to tell Isis how much I love her. I knew I was gonna let her go, but I needed to have one last moment with her before I did. Minutes later, I told her she could go.

Once Isis was gone, my heart was racing and pounding through my chest. My body was shaking, I was confused, I couldn't think straight, and I was angry—an out-of-body experience. Again, something took over me. I went to the kitchen and grabbed a knife. I was ready to go outside to kill Denise or get killed by the police.

So many thoughts and rage were going through my mind all at once. It was overwhelming. In the moment, I thought about taking my own life but Jahad kept appearing in my mind. I was nauseous, lightheaded. I blacked out for a few minutes. I was in and out of consciousness. Scared because I didn't understand what was happening to me. I played back what just happened in my head over and over again. I felt sick. I wanted to die, but I knew I needed to find strength for Jahad's sake. I knew he needed me and it would be selfish of me to get locked up or take my own life. I eventually cried myself asleep. It's now been four years since I've had any contact with Isis. Parental alienation is child abuse. The end.

"Make no mistake, if a child is rejecting a loving parent, they are being abused! Not by the parent they are rejecting, but by the parent who is covertly coercing the rejection. Kids don't reject a parent; kids love both parents. Manipulating a child to hate their mother or father is one of the most despicable things a human being can do and should be made punishable in the court of the law."

– Unknown

"Every morning a parent mourns the loss of a child who is still alive because not seeing the child feels like death."

– Unknown

To the thousands of erased parents out there, I know your pain. People on the outside will never understand what we went through and what we're going through. Please keep hope alive and know that one day we will reunite with our child/children. Parental alienation can lead to post-traumatic stress disorder (PTSD), depression, nightmares, anxiety, panic attacks, suicide, and, unfortunately, murder. Don't be afraid to seek help from a mental health professional if you are experiencing these things.

If you are currently in a relationship, engaged, or married and are planning to have children, please understand you are not exempt from parental alienation. It can happen to you. In the event of a break-up or divorce, please know that it's in your child's best interest to have a healthy, consistent relationship with both parents, especially if both parents are mentally stable.

Imagine how many children we could save if parental alienation was publicly spread throughout the news, social media, family court, child protective services, and all educational outlets. Imagine how many alienated children, who are now adults, never had the opportunity to be a part of their other parent's life because of all the lies, control, and manipulation by the alienating parent.

Imagine how it feels to be the child in the middle of this crisis. Imagine the child's mindset as they're being emotionally forced to turn against the other parent that they equally love. Imagine being put in a situation to have to pick a side.

Dear alienating parent,

Your child isn't choosing you because they love you more; they're choosing you because your love is conditional and they know it. They choose you out of fear. The fear of losing your love.

Dear targeted parent,

Your child is rejecting you because your love is unconditional and they know you will ALWAYS be there, even if it hurt you. Your child rejects you out of fear of the alienating parent, not fear of you. You are safe. You are secure.

There are no winners here, only losers, and the child loses the most.

– Unknown

If you're an alienated child, please know that it's not your fault. One day you will grow up and realize that you were alienated and it's never too late to reunite with the other parent if they are still living. One day you will tell your story of what you went through emotionally—the pain and confusion, how you managed to deal with it from within, and how you overcame it. It will become part of someone else's survival guide.

My Child Did Exist

I've lost a child, I hear myself say,
and the person I'm talking to just turns
away. Now why did I tell them, I don't
understand, It wasn't to get sympathy or to
get a helping hand.
I just want them to know I've lost something
dear, I want them to know my child was here.
My child left something behind which no
one can see, so if I've upset you, I'm sorry
as I can be.
You'll have to forgive me, I could not
resist, I just want you to know that
my child did exist.

~Author Unknown

About the Author

Kenyada Jones is a loving father of two children, a speaker, an entrepreneur, and a parental rights activist. Kenyada's mission is to continue to research the root of parental alienation and determine ways to prevent it. Kenyada's mission is to provide support to all children and parents who are affected by it and educate society about parental alienation, which Kenyada believes should be defined as child abuse.